Journey From Religion to Relationship

Amazing events from New Zealand to America

Delwyn Beveridge

e-Book ISBN: 978-1-966414-10-0

Paperback ISBN: 978-1-966414-11-7

Hardcover ISBN: 978-1-966414-12-4

DEDICATION

This Book is dedicated to my beloved husband Paul and to
our four children.

Sarah, Daniel, Jemima and Priscilla.

TABLE OF CONTENTS

INTRODUCTION

Having lived in three different countries, I've been blessed to meet and connect with people from all walks of life. No matter where I go, someone inevitably asks, "Where are you from?" Some try to guess—often landing on "Australia?"—and it always leads to a conversation. Over the years, I've shared many of my miracle stories in groups, house meetings, and churches. Time and again, people have said to me, "You should write a book." Well—here it is!

As a minister, teacher, and counselor, I've had the unique opportunity to witness both Christian and secular cultures up close. I've also walked through the challenges of being caught in restrictive, legalistic environments that can stifle spiritual growth. One of the main themes of this book is my journey in discerning the difference between a genuine relationship with God and simply conforming to the expectations of religious authorities or rigid rule-keeping.

God has given every person a measure of faith—the capacity to believe Him. Yet I've met many who feel broken and disillusioned because of harmful theology, misguided preaching, and unrealistic expectations. I never wanted to throw out the "baby with the bathwater." What I longed for was a real, living relationship with God—one that was personal, vibrant, and rooted in truth. I wanted scripture to come alive within me, and I wanted to know, without a doubt, that God is real—beyond the bounds of organized religion.

Together with my husband, Paul, our journey has taken us from New Zealand, through Canada, and eventually to the United States. Along the way, we've discovered firsthand what God can do when we choose to believe His Word—even in the face of challenging circumstances.

If organized religion or past disappointments have caused you to turn away from faith, I pray that as you read this book, your heart will be stirred and your faith renewed. God loves you—and He is more than able to keep you.

CHAPTER 1.

HOW I MET MY LIFE PARTNER.

I was born in Dunedin, New Zealand, to Christian-conservative parents. My parents encouraged me in every way, and led by example that I would grow in the Grace and knowledge of Jesus Christ. They taught me that faith wasn't just something we talked about on Sundays but something we lived every day, through kindness, forgiveness, and unwavering trust in God's plan.

When I was 18 years old, I went to our Easter church youth camp at Pleasant Valley, Otago, with the idea that this camp would be different from the others, in that I would not go to find a new boyfriend, but rather to seek a sincere deeper relationship with God. I prayed for clarity and asked God to guide my heart toward His purpose for my life.

At the end of each day, it was the custom to take one's coffee mug and walk up the hill to the kitchen for hot chocolate to take to cabin devotions. When I got to the end of the line, Paul Beveridge was the person in front of me. We had met casually from time to time at various provincial church activities. Something about that night felt different, almost as if an unseen hand had gently nudged us together. I first noticed Paul at a church activity when I was fifteen. He stood out from the crowd, because he wore a leather jacket, and I thought he looked like Elvis Presley. I asked someone about him, and was told he came from Canada. At fifteen, boys were not really on my radar.

We soon became reacquainted and Paul invited me to go to his church cabin for evening devotions. I felt a quiet excitement, sensing that God might be orchestrating something special.

He offered to walk me back to my cabin after we had shared in his Oamaru church devotional time.

We sat under a tree and talked nonstop. The time was slipping by and we didn't notice that lots of time had passed. We shared stories, hopes, and dreams, as if we had known each other forever. Once I finally returned to my cabin, I was informed that I was in trouble for not returning on time. Apparently, Paul was told the same thing when he returned to his cabin.

The next morning at Breakfast in the camp common room, my name and Paul's name were called out, and given the task of cleaning the cook's pots for the remainder of the camp. Well, that just put us together to do a task. Paul was very apologetic and claimed responsibility for our punishment. **He said to me, "Delwyn, I will do the cleaning of the pots and pans. I don't want you to do anything but just talk to me."** His kindness and willingness to sacrifice his comfort for mine touched my heart in a way I couldn't quite explain. As we talked, we shared how we each came to have a relationship with Jesus, and how we both wanted to grow closer to Him. Paul shared how he had also decided that at this camp, he would focus on spiritual things. It felt like God had brought us together to encourage each other in our faith.

This led to our first real date, when Paul came down to Dunedin to attend the Polytech for his studies in Building Science. Each time Paul came down to visit me, he brought me a little bouquet of sweetheart roses. Our dating was wonderful and spread over three years. Each visit felt like a gift, a reminder that love, when rooted in faith, grows patiently and beautifully.

Paul was and still is, a perfect match for me. He is a rock-solid yet gentle type of man, who is not nearly as talkative as me. He did not come from a communicative family, as I did. During our dating years, and even after marriage, Paul was in the New Zealand Army and was often away at army training. We had so many great discussions, many of them by letters. My letters were always long. Writing letters became a sacred ritual. A way to pour our hearts onto paper, bridging the distance with words.

During the time that Paul was away in the army, there was another young medical student, David, who became a very good friend. There was no romance involved, although I think because I was involved with Paul, any romance was kept at bay. David knew Paul and knew that he liked to smoke. David wasted no time in challenging me to confront Paul and ask him to give up smoking since I was not used to having a smoker in my family. David asked me if I would want Paul to smoke if I was to be married to him. Of course, the answer was 'no'. I decided to write to Paul and ask him if he would give up smoking for me, otherwise we wouldn't have a future. It wasn't an easy letter to write, but I trusted that honesty would strengthen our bond.

A letter from Paul came quickly, where he assured me that he had no choice but to give up smoking. Meanwhile, Paul's mother phoned me within a few days of my receiving his letter, to invite me to come to Oamaru as a surprise for Paul as he had been given an out-of-schedule, weekend off. Of course, I wanted to do this. I arrived in Oamaru by bus and was welcomed by Paul's mother who knew nothing of my letter to Paul. She explained that I should stand behind the drape in their living room and surprise Paul as he came in the door. My heart raced with anticipation, imagining his face when he saw me. I did as we planned, and very soon we could hear Paul coming in the door. He was in army uniform, with a bag in one hand, and a cigarette in the other! My heart sank for a moment, but I reminded myself that change is a process, not an instant decision. I appeared from behind the drape to welcome him, but we both saw at the same time that he was smoking. "Ok, you've caught me," Paul said. The moment was awkward, but I decided not to talk about it in front of his mother. The talk took place later, and the infamous cigarette, was the last one Paul ever smoked. It became a turning point, a testament to his commitment to our future. The benefits of dating, bring out issues that still give time to decide on options.

Paul told me that his dad would not allow him to be water baptized, because he had been christened as a baby. He waited until he was twenty-one to be baptized so that his dad could not object. I attended Paul's baptism in the Oamaru Baptist church. It was a wonderful occasion, and the baptizer, was an intern pastor, Don Dickson. Watching Paul publicly declare his faith deepened my love and respect for him even more.

During our dating time, I was a newly qualified Elementary school teacher, doing country service in a two-teacher school in Becks, Central Otago. I used to come home at weekends because my mother was very lonely, having lost my father just two years before. During this time, I would return to Becks by railcar on a Sunday afternoon. On one of these railcar trips, Don Dickson happened to be in my carriage, going to Alexandra in Central Otago. I sat next to him and we had a great conversation about dating and marriage. Don was newly married at the time, and knew my family, and knew that Paul and I were dating. I asked Don, "How does a person know when it's the right one?" He gave me a very wise reply. He said, "Ask yourself these three questions. 1. Do you mutually truly love each other? 2. Has your relationship passed the test of time? 3. Does your relationship bring glory to God?" If you can say "yes" to all three questions, you have found the right one.

Our dating continued between Oamaru and Dunedin, until our engagement on New Year's Eve 1965, and our wedding on December 3rd of 1966. It felt like the culmination of everything we had prayed for — a love story written by God Himself. The night before our wedding, guests were coming to the front door to give wedding gifts. I went to the door to answer the doorbell and there stood my medical student friend, David. He handed me a gift and said to me, "I hope Paul will make you as happy as I would have liked to." I thanked him and wished him well. There was no regret, as I was totally in love with Paul. David went on to marry and was very successful in his life. The gift he gave me, was a pearl-handled carving set, which Paul still jokes about. We still use it. Every time we use that carving set, we smile, knowing that life's twists and turns always lead us exactly where we're meant to be.

Matthew 6 verse 33, says "Seek first the kingdom of God and His righteousness, and all these other things will be added unto you." Paul and I had individually decided to seek the Lord that particular Easter camp, three years earlier, and He gave us to each other..........Life Partners.

CHAPTER 2.

THE BLESSING OF CHILDREN.

In our early marriage, Paul and I were involved with Youth for Christ amongst other youth ministries. We particularly enjoyed counseling and mentoring young people who were new Christians. The leaders of Youth for Christ who trained us, came to our house one night and challenged us. They told us that if we were going to counsel couples with children, then it would be better to wait until we had children of our own to have more experience. Their words weighed heavily on our hearts, but we trusted that God would guide us in the right direction. After much discussion, Paul and I decided that we would pray about this and possibly start a family. Growing up, I had one brother who was older than me. I longed for a sister, but even in my youth, I had in my heart that someday, I would love to have 4 children so they could play together. Paul shared this view with me. A few weeks later, I stopped taking the "pill" and we knelt down together beside our bed. We prayed and dedicated ourselves to the Lord. I remember feeling an overwhelming sense of peace as if God was already working behind the scenes. I remember putting in my requests that my children would grow to know and love the Lord, but I also expressed that if there was a reason God knew best, I would be content to be childless.

Time went by, and my assumption that I would have a baby soon became intense. The signs were all there, and off I went to the doctor. After an examination, the doctor informed me that I was not pregnant. The words hit me like a wave, and I felt my heart sink. I found it hard to accept. I came home very upset and forgot that I had prayed that it would be ok to not have children. I was crying way too much and began to feel ashamed of being so upset over the situation. I went into my bedroom to pray to ask the Lord to correct my thinking. I pleaded with God, pouring out all my sadness and confusion. This is when it happened. Suddenly, as I was praying and wiping up my tears of disappointment, I heard a loud male voice over my right shoulder say, "Read Galatians 4." I turned to see who spoke, but no one was there. It was awesome, powerful, and very real. My whole body tingled as I realized I had just experienced something divine. I thought it must be the Lord or an angel, and I tried to remember if Galatians 4 was about the fruit of the Spirit. I was reading from my Living Bible at the time and I quickly turned to Galatians 4.

My eyes began to read verse 27 "Now you can rejoice O childless woman, you can shout with joy though you never before had a child. For I am going to give you many children—more than the slave wife has." What an encounter that was!!!!

Shout for joy is exactly what I did. I felt like chains of doubt had broken off me, and hope flooded my heart. Now I knew that I would have children. How many is "many" we will talk about later. This was a supernatural experience.

The passage this scripture was about concerned Sarah, Abraham's wife. She was a Godly woman and was known for her beauty. Paul and I decided, that if our first baby was a girl, she would be named Sarah. It felt like a prophetic declaration, and we clung to that promise with all our faith.

Very soon after this, I became sick and the doctor informed me that I was indeed pregnant and that his first diagnosis had been wrong. God's word had come to life, and we were overwhelmed with gratitude.

The time came for the birth. Back in those days, no mother knew what gender the baby would be. I was given an anesthetic because the baby needed a high forceps delivery, called a Keilland's Rotation. Paul was there and the first to learn the baby was a healthy girl. He tried to tell me that we have a girl but I was totally out. So Paul whispered in my ear "Sarah's arrived." Out of my spirit, I replied, "Praise the Lord!" Even in a state of unconsciousness, my soul rejoiced. In Queen Mary Hospital at that time, it was 3 days before I was allowed to see Sarah. But what a beautiful baby!!! She had no marks at all from the forceps, no swelling, just a totally beautiful baby. I was so thrilled. She was perfect, and I couldn't stop thanking God for His faithfulness.

CHAPTER 3.

PROMISES CHALLENGED

Sarah was seven months old when I noticed that my waist was filling out. Everything else was normal. I was home alone at the time because Paul was at a Building Law class. Suddenly searing pain went through me which forced me to the ground. I called our family doctor, Doctor Wyatt, who had delivered Sarah. After answering his questions, he suggested I was having an ectopic pregnancy and needed to get to the hospital immediately. Fear tried to grip me, but I held onto God's promise, whispering prayers for strength. Paul was contacted at the college by my mother and he came home to get me right away. I was admitted to a hospital where doctors determined that I was indeed pregnant with the fetus growing in the wrong place. This meant that I needed immediate lifesaving surgery.

After the surgery was over, the doctors came to talk to me and informed me that they had to remove one ovary and one fallopian tube. Additionally, they said that my remaining fallopian tube was also blocked and that in all likelihood, I would not conceive again. It sounded like all hope was lost, but deep inside I knew that nothing is impossible with God. It's times like this when it is so important to think with the mind of Christ, which is the Word. When the doctors told me their statement, the Spirit of God reminded me of His statement, and I replied, "No, you'll see, I will have more children, I know I will." My words felt like a declaration of war against doubt, and I knew heaven was listening.

Twenty-three months later, a perfect baby boy was born to us. We named him Daniel. The faithfulness of God…Romans 3 v 4 "Let God be true, but every man a liar."

"Daniel" was the name we chose while I was pregnant, because of the inspiration we received while reading the book of Daniel, and the verse that captured us, was Daniel chapter 1 v 17. {NLT} "God gave these four young men an unusual aptitude for understanding every aspect of literature and wisdom and God gave Daniel the special ability to interpret the meanings of visions and dreams." In the years that followed, these words would be made clear. Every time I held Daniel, I felt like I was holding a living, breathing miracle.

Paul and I had discussed how many children were "many," and we decided that two was some, three was a few, but four had to mean "many." So now, all we had to do was have two more. We laughed as we dreamed, knowing that the same God who had already done the impossible could do it again. However, Psalm 105 v 19, says "Until the time that His word came: The word of the Lord tried him." We didn't know it yet, but our faith would be tested again and God's faithfulness would shine even brighter.

CHAPTER 4.

THE WAIT FOR NUMBERS THREE AND FOUR

Two years went by, with no sign of the number three. I found it encouraging to thank the Lord for His promise and to say aloud to myself whenever I thought of it, that "two more children are coming." Some days were harder than others, especially when I longed to hold another baby in my arms. But I clung to faith, reminding myself that God's timing is always perfect.

Paul and I took turns to stay home with the children whenever we both needed to be somewhere. One Wednesday night when I was on music duty at our church, I left home to attend the mid-week meeting. It was a very warm evening, and during the meeting, everyone could hear the wind getting up outside. Trash can lids could be heard banging around outside. Suddenly, the power went out and everyone was advised to leave. Up until then, the meeting had been very inspiring with a great time singing various scriptures to music.

Outside, everything was dark. No streetlights were on. I was driving home carefully and noticed police cars were appearing in the streets. The wind was raging and at one point, I was redirected by police to a detour because of a huge fallen tree across the road. I whispered prayers of protection as I navigated the unfamiliar route, trusting God to guide me home safely. I made my way to Highcliff Road, which was the road we lived on. I made my way slowly because other than my car lights, everything was dark, loud, and creepy outside.

Suddenly, after a huge gust of wind, my car was entangled with wires that came down and wrapped themselves around my car. My car was now stationary, and I saw flames beginning to burn the rubber around my windshield. I thought my car might explode. At that time, I had very little if any, knowledge of electricity. All I thought of, was that I must get out of the car before it explodes. I did not know that as soon as my foot touched the ground while opening the door, I would be electrocuted. My heart was pounding, and for a moment, fear gripped me. But then, I remembered who my protector was.

I sat for a moment to pray. The words of a song we had sung in church that night from the book of Ruth 3 v 9 in the Bible, came back to me. I prayed" Lord, as I get out of the car, "cover me, and spread the border of your garment over me," I can't die because I haven't had my other two children yet." I had no idea how fast the wind was, nor did I consider that I wouldn't be able to stand and cross the road. I was able to open the car door a little, just as a huge gust of wind blew every wire off my car in a straight line, even with pieces of metal on the end of it.

As I stepped out, there was a man's hand right there to grab mine. This man had formed a chain with other neighbors when they saw what was happening to me. Their faces, illuminated by flashlights, looked like angels sent to rescue me. I knew God had orchestrated this moment. I was pulled to the side of the road and looked back at my car. The wires were back all over it, and were only off during the time I got out. What a miracle! The neighbors were out to look at what was going on with the storm just at that time. I expressed my gratitude to them and inwardly praised God for the power of His word and His promise to me. Psalm 138 v 2 says "The Lord honors His word above His name."

Meanwhile, I continually sought the Lord about becoming pregnant again. Each month that passed without a positive sign tested my patience, but I tried to focus on His faithfulness rather than my frustration.

I found so much comfort and leading in Isaiah, and usually read from The Living Bible. One day, as I was reading from Isaiah 54, verses 2 and 3 just came alive to me.

"Enlarge your house; build on additions; spread out your home! For you will soon be bursting at the seams! At the time, our home was a simple rancher with three bedrooms. I showed Paul the scriptures, and we discussed this thoroughly.

With Paul's knowledge of building science, we discussed how an addition could be possible. Paul studied the house plans and found a way that a second story could be added to our home if we used one of the current bedrooms to put a staircase in. It felt like a step of faith, expanding our home even before the children came, but we trusted that God was leading us. It wasn't long before we had the paperwork completed, hired a builder, and the addition was underway.

The top story on our house took six months to complete. The addition gave us five bedrooms as well as other living spaces. I was getting desperate, and I was sure the Lord was tired of me asking Him "When am I going to have the next baby? I was constantly aware, that I had heard the audible voice of the Lord, who had told me that I would have many children, according to Galatians 4 v 27.

Our church often had guest speakers, and one Sunday, a man from the United States was the speaker. We always loved to hear anyone from America. This man was traveling around the world to talk about his near-death experience of twenty minutes, when he died and came back into his body. He claimed that during the time he was out of his body, God gave him gifts to know future events and other issues. Both Paul and I were fascinated. Once the church service was over, we asked this man if he would like to come to our home for lunch. He was delighted, and so we took him home with us. It was a cold New Zealand winter day in August that year.

I shared with this godly man about the time the Lord had spoken aloud to me, nearly three years ago. He looked at me very intently, and declared "You will have a baby next year." Of course, I was delighted, because this meant that I could conceive any time and the baby would be born the next year. I received his word for me and believed him. I calculated, that the latest I could conceive and still have the baby the next year, would be March of the following year. My heart soared with renewed hope, and I felt like God was gently reminding me He hadn't forgotten His promise.

I was very excited. The next two babies were now in sight. I wanted to have a special time alone with the Lord to thank Him for this encouragement. I was reading my favorite book, Isaiah, when I read this verse in chapter 51 v 3. The Prophet Isaiah was talking in this chapter to Israel. However, when the word comes alive as you read it, it becomes a Rhema word, which is when God is speaking it to you, and it's personal. It felt like God Himself was whispering hope directly to my heart.

"The Lord will bless you again, and make your deserts blossom; your barren wilderness will become as beautiful as the Garden of Eden. Joy and gladness will be found there, **Thanksgiving, and Lovely Songs.**" I knew that soon, my waiting would be over. I was forgetting, that there is an enemy of our faith, the devil, who does everything possible to try to cause us to doubt the Lord and especially doubt His promises. The devil uses thoughts of doubt, circumstances, and lying symptoms. But I held on, determined that no matter what the enemy tried, my faith would stand strong. My babies were coming, and I trusted God to fulfill His word.

Six months went by, and no sign of any pregnancy. Each passing day tested my faith, but I clung tightly to the Lord's promise, whispering prayers in quiet moments and reminding myself that God's timing is perfect. By now, it is

February of the next year. One day, a special letter arrived from the New Zealand Military for Paul. At this point, Paul had been in the Military on reserve, for six years after his first three doing full-time service. Paul opened the letter and shared the contents with me. It was an invitation to go on a promotional training opportunity for the Army. The course would extend for six weeks, with the payment of a large sum of money. Our hearts wrestled with the decision, torn between the practical need for finances and the spiritual conviction that God's promise was near. We discussed this opportunity with gratitude because the money was much needed at the time and very attractive. We didn't like the idea of being separated for six weeks, but we thought it would be worth it. Then, the Spirit of God began to remind me, that I had to conceive by March, for baby number three to be born by the end of that year. For Paul to be away for six weeks at that time, would present a choice for us to consider. It was a defining moment. A test of trust. Do we believe that the Lord told us I would have a baby by the end of that year? Or do we take this opportunity to advance in the Army and have some much-needed money?

We chose to believe the Lord and turned down the opportunity from the Military. It was a leap of faith, a decision that felt like stepping off a cliff and trusting God to catch us. March thirty first, was my deadline to conceive.

In those days, I had the one family car at home, and Paul caught a bus to work. It was Paul's habit, to read The Daily Light, which was a devotional, written by Billy Graham's daughter, with daily readings for morning and evening. On April 1, Paul had left the page open where he left it on the table. As the day wore on, I discovered that I had my "monthly." March had come and gone, and huge disappointment was setting in on me. It felt like my heart shattered into pieces, and the weight of discouragement pressed heavily on my chest. Did I cry? Of course, I did. I also prayed and told the Lord that what I was experiencing, was a cruel joke. April the first, April Fool's Day of all days! The irony of the date stung like salt in a wound, and for a brief moment, doubt tried to overshadow my hope. As I thought about the meaning of April fool, I decided to read the page Paul had left open for April first in the Daily Light Devotional. I began to read in the evening section. I remember, that the text was from Isaiah chapter 9, but I do not know which translation it was. The opening sentence said, **"Surely, a son shall be born unto you."** It was a reference to the fact that Jesus would come. However, to me, it was the greatest comfort of all, that yes, I will have a baby!

Tears of sadness turned to tears of hope as I clutched the Bible to my chest, feeling God's presence so intimately.

Several days went by, and I was feeling very sick. At first, I dismissed it as stress, but deep inside, a tiny spark of hope flickered. My family doctor examined me and informed me that I was about six weeks pregnant. He explained that what I had experienced, was related to when the placenta shifts, and if it hadn't moved when it did, I might have had a miscarriage. My heart pounded as his words sank in. God had not only fulfilled His promise but had protected the life growing inside me. This meant, that this pregnancy had been conceived exactly when Paul would have been away in Army training, had he accepted the opportunity. Exercising faith and believing the Lord leaves no disappointment. The devil had given me lying symptoms in an attempt to cause me to mistrust the word of the Lord and stop believing Him. Even though I was very disappointed on April 1, the grace of God supplied encouragement for me. His grace lifted me out of despair and replaced my sorrow with overflowing joy.

The doctor informed me, that this baby would be expected in late November of that year. Amazing and wonderful. Faithful is the Lord God Almighty!

Jemima arrived safely on November twenty-second, 1974. In the event that the baby might be a girl, we chose her name from the book of Job in the Bible, chapter 42, v 13, 14, and 15. "God gave Job three more daughters, and their names were Jemima, Kezia, and Keren. In all the land, there were no other girls as lovely as the daughters of Job; and they were all in their father's will." It felt like a prophetic name. A reminder of God's restoration and His promise to bless us abundantly. We had no idea at all, that in 1986, we would be living in The United States, and Jemima's birthday, would fall during the week of THANKSGIVING! It was as if God aligned her life with a season of gratitude, to always remind us of His faithfulness.

While I was in the Maternity Hospital after Jemima's birth, I went down to the common room to talk to other mothers. There was one lady in the room who was very distressed and nervously smoking. After talking with her, she told me that her previous baby had died of SIDS, not long after it was born. She explained that she was very anxious and afraid that her new baby would suffer the same fate. Her words pierced my heart, and a wave of fear tried to creep in. I comforted her as best I could, but talking with her caused me to begin to have fearful thoughts for Jemima. I headed back to my room to pray that God would reassure me after all that had happened, that Jemima would not die of SIDS.

Once again, I opened my Living Bible to Isaiah, and it opened in chapter 44. Verses 3 and 4 stood out to me. "I will pour out my Spirit and my blessings on your children. They shall thrive like watered grass, like willows on a river bank. 'I am the Lord's," they'll proudly say! Tears of relief streamed down my face. God had already given me the promise. Jemima would not just live, she would thrive. My heart was greatly at peace for this amazing reassurance. I did not know at that time, just how vital these verses would be. I have learned in life, that when God speaks to my spirit, I need to get it in writing. The Spirit and the Word are in agreement.

! Peter 5 v 8 describes the devil as a hungry lion, looking for some victim to tear apart. But as always, the Lord has help and encouragement for us. Psalm 34 v19 says "Many are the afflictions of the righteous, but the Lord delivers him out of them all!" Those words became a shield for my heart. Every attack of fear was met with the truth of God's promises.

When Jemima was three months old, I took her to our family doctor for her first vaccinations. In those days, patients came into the doctor's room, and procedures were carried out on a bed with a grey woolen blanket on it. I have no idea how often the blanket was changed. Jemima was placed on the blanket face down ready for her vaccination. She was moving her little mouth all over the blanket, looking for milk. All seemed normal until the next day. Jemima began screaming uncontrollably and her diaper was filled with blood. My heart shattered at the sight of her pain. It felt like the enemy was launching another attack. The hospital soon discovered that she had Typhosa Maria, a notifiable disease. It was discovered that the disease had come from the doctor's room where the previous patient had been, who was found to have the disease. Not only was Jemima the youngest person to ever have this disease in New Zealand, but because of this situation, all doctors changed to rolling paper sheets which are changed after each patient.

Jemima remained very ill and could only drink potato milk. Each day felt like a battlefield, and we clung to hope like a lifeline. There were days when she looked almost transparent and we wondered if she would die. Paul and I took turns to leave the house. One Sunday morning, I went to church. The pastor was speaking about the Old Testament practice of sacrifices and its meaning. As I went to go home after the service, the pastor came to me. He knew about

Jemima. He thought it necessary to say to me, "Now Delwyn, if the Lord takes Jemima, are you going to stop following the Lord?" His words felt like a punch to my spirit I didn't answer him. As I ran out the door, a fellow musician and friend, quickly gave me a scripture to look up when I got home. I drove home crying and ran into the house to tell Paul what the pastor had said. Paul was resolute. He said firmly, "Jemima will not die, and God doesn't take people anyway. He receives them, but the Lord gave her to us and we won't let the devil take her." His unwavering faith became my anchor in that storm. I remembered the scripture that my friend had given me. I usually read from my Living Bible and knew he had said Psalm 50. I began to read it, knowing God's word is powerful. I came to verse. "But it isn't sacrificial bullocks that I want from you. All the animals are mine! The cattle on a thousand hills! v13-15 What I want from you, is your true thanks; I want you to trust me in your times of trouble, so I can rescue you and you can give me glory."

Wow! Paul and I praised the Lord for how wonderful He is and how Faithful. It was as if heaven itself broke through our despair, flooding us with hope. Jemima began to get better from that day forward. The Lord had given me the promise at her birth that she would thrive like a willow on the river bank. And now, that promise was blooming right before our eyes. God had not only saved her but used her life as a testimony of His goodness and miraculous power.

CHAPTER 5.

BABY NUMBER FOUR

My doctor had told me that my body was reacting to each pregnancy as if the baby was an allergy to my body. This was evidenced by the increasing nausea and additional before and after difficulties I had experienced. The feeling of exhaustion, nausea, and discomfort felt almost unbearable at times, and every pregnancy seemed to make the symptoms worse. Thirteen months after Jemima's birth, I was pregnant with number four. I was experiencing a great deal of sickness and breathing problems. Since the four promised children were almost complete, Paul and I waited until the first trimester was over, and then we made the medical decision to ensure that there would be no more pregnancies.. Paul took care of that!!

By the time I was four and a half months on with the pregnancy, I couldn't keep water down, and couldn't breathe. I was hospitalized for two weeks on various treatments via IV, and finally, one afternoon when Paul was beside my bed visiting me, three doctors came into my room to talk to us. They discussed that the solution to my case, was a legal abortion. This was totally unacceptable to us. The thought of ending this pregnancy was unbearable, especially after all we had gone through.

This was our fourth promised baby and we couldn't have another one. We told the doctors that they had to come up with some other idea or drug, because this baby was going to full term. After the doctors left us, Paul prayed with me and encouraged me to be affirming in my mind and heart, the words I had heard from the audible voice before Sarah was born. I said them over and over as I could. "You will give me many children Lord. Thank you. This baby is one of them".

A couple of days later, a doctor came to me to see if I would try an experimental drug that would possibly enable me to breathe, which would then in turn if working, help me to keep fluids down. I was all for it. After a day or two, the drug began to work, and I was sent home. Praise the Lord!!

The days following my discharge were filled with both relief and cautious hope. While the new medication gave me the ability to breathe and hold down fluids, each moment still felt fragile. I leaned heavily on prayer and the promises I had received from the Lord. Every small improvement was a reason to be thankful, and though my strength returned slowly, my spirit was lifted knowing this baby—our fourth and final promise—was being carried toward full term. We took things one day at a time, trusting that God, who had already done so much for us, would bring this child safely into the world.

Despite the difficulties, Priscilla was born safely, twenty-two months after Jemima. From the time Priscilla could talk, she began to sing. Every night on going to sleep, she would sing in her bed and the songs were lovely. Her voice was so pure and sweet that it would fill the whole house with peace. LOVELY SONGS She continues to be a lovely singer.

CHAPTER 6.

A PERSONAL CRISIS!

These were wonderful happy days. The family was complete, along with one dog. All the children were healthy, and doing well. Paul and I hungered for more of the Lord. We wanted to be fed and taught. A man in our church owned a Bible book store. We asked him if he had any new books from America. He told us that he had just received a box of books from Tulsa, but nothing new except for a magazine that advertised new books. We asked him if we could borrow the magazine. The magazine advertised a book on the back called 'THE CONFESSIONS OF A BAPTIST PREACHER' written by John Osteen. It was a manual for using the sword of the spirit which is the word of God in spiritual combat. I decided to order this book.

By the time Priscilla was six weeks old, we decided to take the family for a vacation to Lake Wanaka. We had friends who gave us their vacation house for a week. While we were there, I began to feel ill and developed a very strange rash. Paul took me to a local doctor, who ordered blood tests and sent a letter to my family doctor back home. The lab had results quickly, and they were given to me in a sealed envelope along with a copy to my family doctor. Of course, I opened the envelope, but I didn't understand what it was about. It seemed to say that I had Leukemia. I couldn't believe it at first. It felt like everything in my world was turning upside down. Once we were home, my doctor asked me to come to see him. I will never forget that appointment. He was reading results from further blood tests that I had. He looked at me across his desk with a very serious face and said, "I'm so sorry Delwyn". That look, and the conversation that followed, put real fear in my heart. I left the doctor's office and went to where Paul worked and told him everything. I said, "Dear, I might die". Paul said with steadfast faith, "I won't let you die, dear". I went home with my mind racing. I thought that maybe we would have to go to America and be prayed for by a pastor in Tulsa. Those were thoughts of fear. Immediately, the Holy Spirit reminded me that any pastor would have to use the power of God which I had access to without going to America.

The Holy Spirit's reminder gave me a renewed sense of peace and confidence. I knew that I didn't have to go anywhere; God was right here with me.

In the mail that day, was the book I had ordered. The very tool I needed to help me. When Paul came home from work that day, I told the family, that no one could comfort me or tell me what I wanted to hear, except God Himself. I needed to find a way to really get into the presence of God to the point that I could reach Him and have Him heal me. With my new book in hand, I declared to the family, "I'm going upstairs to the family room, and I'm not coming back until I'm healed".

It never occurred to me that God wouldn't heal me. I knew that if I could get close enough to Him, that He would heal me…. And so began an amazing experience!

I went into the family room, closed the door, and knelt to pray at the sofa in the room. I knew the words of Hebrews 11 v 6, He is a rewarder of those that diligently seek Him". I was aware that I was fearful and I had to reverse the fear with faith. I began to pray, but I couldn't sense God's presence at all. The fear was still there, trying to cling to me, but I pressed on with faith. My mind was whirling around with words the doctor had said and my own fear of leaving the family.

I knew that my only hope was to actually really believe the promises of God in the Word. I also had my New King James Bible with me and I opened it to read in Isaiah 43 v 26. "Put me in remembrance; Let us contend together, state your case, that you may be acquitted". I opened John

Osteen's book to chapter 10 entitled "A Confession of Victory over Fear". I began to read it out loud. The words seemed to be empty to me, because the thoughts from the devil, were so strong. The battle in my mind was fierce, but I kept speaking the truth of God's Word, refusing to let fear have the final say. I knew that faith comes from hearing the word of God. I began to pray scripture to the Lord as I remembered various verses. "Lord, you said in your word, that you are a rewarder of those that diligently seek you. Well, here I am, diligently seeking you. You said in Psalm 103, that you heal all my diseases. You said in Jeremiah 29 v 11, that you had plans to prosper me and not harm me, and plans to give me a hope and a future". I was stating my case based on the promises of God, provided in His Word. At this point, all I was doing was hard work. My emotions were still very uneasy. But I knew that this was the work of faith, and I wasn't going to give up. I began to read John Osteen's book aloud. It was written with scriptures in the first person, so that they were as affirmations. As I read these, I varied them with my own scriptures as they came to my remembrance.

'In Philippians 2 v 9 & 10, you said that your name is above every name. That means Lord that your name is above leukemia, and at your name, leukemia must bow." I began to feel the Spirit of God deep inside me as I quoted these promises aloud. Faith was beginning to stir. I continued," Lord you said in Psalm 23, that you are my shepherd and I won't lack. Well, that means that I won't lack for healing. You also said in Psalm 91, that you would satisfy me with long life, and show me your salvation." At this point, I was feeling bold and as I continued to plead my case to the Lord, I began to feel my mind being filled with a powerful sense of the Holy Spirit. Then something happened, which I can only explain after the fact, as I reflect back on it. I didn't know at the time, but it was an out of body experience. I found myself in a high place on a cantilevered platform. It seemed to be a courtroom. A smoke like substance was rising from under the platform and going upwards. I was aware that to my left was a throne, but I couldn't see any more to my left. I saw these curled fingernails over the edge of the platform coming from underneath. Jesus was standing over to my right, facing towards my left. A voice from over by the fingernails began to speak. I knew it was the devil and he was the council for the Prosecution. The devil began to level many accusations towards me. He was accusing me of things I had been forgiven for years ago. He was saying that I deserved to have leukemia, that I lacked true faith, and that I deserved to die. He seemed to be repeating a lot of the thoughts I had when I first started to pray. Then, Jesus turned to face me. He said nothing, but I knew He was my council for Defense. Everything I was seeing was like a movie. Although Jesus didn't say a word audibly, I was able to hear what He was saying. Although silent, Jesus was representing all the scripture I had been praying. I was speaking the truth. The Word is truth. I knew I was winning my case. The fingernails disappeared. There was an awesome atmosphere. I was aware that someone stood up from the throne to my left. I knew it was God. I could see outstretched hands. I heard two words in a powerful voice. "Case dismissed". I knew I was healed. Then I was back in the family room beside the sofa. I was overcome with emotions of gratitude. I would say that I was in the family room for about three hours. I went back down to the kitchen where Paul was. I declared, "I am healed". I told the family everything that had happened. It was easy to arrange blood tests through my doctor the next day. The doctor wanted several tests. The results were all clear and negative. I owe my life to the power of God's Word. Psalm 107 v 20 says, 'He sent His word and healed them". The Living Bible puts it this way, "He spoke, and they were healed, snatched from the door of death". I have learned, that only faith which comes from believing the word, can reverse fear. Without this truth, it's like a shark named, "The thing you fear", and the pilot fish named "fear' which guides the shark to fulfill the fear. John 8v32 says 'you will know the truth, and the truth will make you free".

CHAPTER 7.

A FAMILY YEARNING FOR MORE OF GOD

Following this wonderful healing experience, Paul and I longed to share what the Lord had done for us. It seemed that when we had the opportunity to share in a small group from our church, the responses were strangely jealous, critical or empty. It was hard to find people who wanted more of God than we wanted. Our pastor had tight control over the church, and others we had tried were similar. Paul heard about a Christian organization that was outside of the control of the local church. It was called Full Gospel Businessmen. Paul began to attend and loved it. He learned that the founders of the Organization, were American, and frequently brought Americans over to be speakers at meetings and conventions. Many of these speakers, were invited by Paul to come to our home for dinner. We had many guests who stayed the night in our guest suite, which was part of the new extensions on our house. America has always been a fascination for us. Our Christmas cards had yuletide logs, snow, and American scenes on them. We didn't think anything of it because the cards were a normal Christmas item everywhere. It didn't occur to us that there was anything wrong with this picture, even though our

Christmas was the middle of summer. We preferred American movies and American humor. Most of all, the best spiritual teaching we heard, was from American speakers, who promoted Jesus as our shepherd, rather than the pastor of the church. Besides, it was an American who had a near-death experience, who had been a big influence in my waiting for the third baby. Also, the book which I sent away for and which was a great tool in my healing, was written by an American author. The magazine which promoted the book, was from Rhema Bible College in Tulsa Oklahoma.

Meanwhile, unknown to us, a man named Dave Soleim in Seattle Washington, was attending a fundraiser for a Jewish organization. The door prize, was a trip for a couple, anywhere in the world for three weeks. Dave Soleim won that prize. Dave happened to be the president of the Seattle chapter of Full Gospel Businessmen. The organization was in the process of planning a trip to New Zealand. Dave and his wife Jackie, decided to use his prize to join this trip. The organization had requirements that the members of the trip were to stay in the homes of local chapter presidents. Dave wanted to go to the Auckland chapters, but they were quickly taken by other members. Dave found himself in Dunedin in the South Island, and was supposed to stay in the chapter president's house. However, the president of the Dunedin chapter happened to be on vacation in Australia. One of the Dunedin members who knew Paul asked him if Dave and Jackie could stay at our place. We were thrilled to have them. During the few days they were with us, we shared deep things with them. Our fellowship was precious and personal. Dave and Jackie sensed our longing to be free from legalistic religion, and cultural stifling, and our longing for more of the freedom we felt when we heard American visiting pastors preach.

The night before Dave and Jackie left to return to Seattle, they made a commitment to pray for us. They felt a lot of love for our family, and said they would pray for the Lord to open new doors for us. We were sad to say goodbye, but we didn't believe that they would pray as they said.

We received a phone call from Dave and Jackie every now and then. We continued in our way of life, but our church situation was so dead. There was no life of the Spirit of God in the services. We felt a continued longing to do something new that would be more fulfilling for serving God.

Meanwhile, I read in the local newspaper, that a lady had to give her dog away, because of a divorce. The situation was urgent for this lady. I badly wanted a dog, but Paul was firmly against this idea. I continued to talk about it to Paul, and finally, he conceded that I could call the lady and ask her more about the dog. This dog was eight years old and a large-sized mixed breed. Paul agreed that we would all go as a family to look at the dog, on condition that I would promise not to bring it home! I was thinking otherwise. It was a funny compromise, but I was determined to convince him. It was clear when we arrived at the lady's house, that Paul did not like the dog. His name was Snoopy, and he was a mix of Point Setter and possibly some other sort of sporting dog. I immediately liked Snoopy, but no amount of pleading could persuade Paul to let me bring him home. The rest of the family went back to the car while I talked with the lady. I told her I was very much wanting Snoopy, but I needed to have time to talk more with Paul, and that I was confident we would be back to get Snoopy. The children were disappointed also. However, I continued to persuade Paul to let me have the dog. I asked him if he would please pray about it. Paul decided to make what he thought was an impossible situation. He said, "Ok, I will pray about it, but unless we hear from the Soleims that Dave has some good news or ideas for us, we should wait. Paul proceeded to walk upstairs to our bedroom to pray about this dog. Paul tells the story like this. "I was on my knees and said to the Lord, "You know how Delwyn wants this dog". The phone rang, interrupting his prayer. Yes, it was Dave Soleim with a wonderful idea. He invited Paul and me to think about going to Los Angeles to the Full Gospel Businessmen's convention next year! Paul came downstairs and told me I could have Snoopy. Two days had gone by and I wondered if Snoopy would still be available. The lady answered the phone and said how happy she was to hear from me, because someone else had wanted the dog, but she remembered how I had said with confidence, that we would be back to get him.

Back we went, and brought Snoopy home with us. It took him a while to bond with us, but I loved him so much and I was his favorite person. We decided to have a family picnic at Outram Glen and include Snoopy. It was a beautiful hot summer day for swimming. We took our gear, inflatable mattress, and of course, games and food. Outram Glen was a very popular place to picnic, because of the river, and the playing fields. After our picnic lunch, Paul and the children set up a net to play badminton. I decided to take the inflatable mattress down to the river to sunbathe on it. The river was a short walk away and down a bank. Conditions for sunbathing were perfect, not a breath of wind. The family was busy having a lot of fun, and I was so relaxed in the sun on the river, that I fell asleep. I had no idea the wind was picking up, . and causing my mattress to drift down the river. At the time I woke up, I found myself a considerable distance from where I had first started. The water had thick green weeds in it and I could not tell how deep it was. The river began to wind around and I remembered that the year before, a man had died trying to rescue his son somewhere on this river near to a whirlpool. I started to yell out as loud as possible," Paul, Help". Paul couldn't hear me, but I kept calling out and grabbing at weeds. Then a miracle happened. Snoopy suddenly appeared running down the bank towards me. He jumped straight into the water and grabbed the half-inch flap of rubber on the side of the mattress. I hung onto his collar and he towed me to the edge of the river where I could get out. By then, Paul had found me, but Snoopy rescued me. I called him 'My hairy brown angel'.

CHAPTER 8.

THE TRIP TO AMERICA

Paul and I discussed at length, the pros and cons of Dave's idea. The year was 1977, and the Full Gospel Businessman's convention was to be held in Los Angeles, in July of 1978. The prospect of going to America was huge for us. We knew about Los Angeles, but we thought if we were going to go that far away, we would want to include a Camp Meeting Convention that was to be held in Tulsa. We had never been to an American Camp Meeting before, and the thought of visiting one filled us with excitement and anticipation. Paul and I knew nothing about an American Camp meeting. We thought we would write to the address on the magazine that advertised the event. The only camp meetings we knew about, were ones we went to in New Zealand for Bible Class camps. In our letter, we asked if we would need to bring a sleeping bag and coffee mug. We received a fairly quick reply which included a hotel guide and application. This opened our ideas up considerably. We had to begin to think like Americans for this event. The Tulsa meeting, would have all our favorite American speakers, and we could include a visit to Seattle, where Dave and Jackie lived. We decided that this would be our plan, as long as my mother would be willing to look after the children in our home, while we were away. For a trip of this magnitude to us, we needed to pray about it. Paul and I talked about how the Lord had told both Joseph and Mary separately that they needed to move to Egypt with Jesus, to ensure they were in agreement. With that in mind, Paul agreed to go upstairs to pray, while I stayed in the kitchen to do the same. I remember that evening very well. I started to pray, but couldn't get into it. Instead, I opened my Living Bible and asked the Lord to give me a scripture of what to do about our plans. I began reading my favorite book Isaiah. I was in chapter 49 when verse 12 stood out to me. It read, "See, my people shall return from far away, from North and West and South" I had no sooner read this, when Paul came down from upstairs. He told me he had finished praying and had peace but nothing more. He hoped that his prayers had helped me to hear from the Lord. I read him my verse from Isaiah. We were so happy, because North, West and South, covered all three areas we wanted to visit. It was the confirmation we had been waiting for. We began to plan how we could afford to pay for our fares. My mother was in agreement to mind the children and Snoopy. We had confirmation from the scripture that we would be returned from far away. Now, it was a matter of praying about how to find the money. We had some savings, but it was not nearly enough. I remembered that Hebrews 11 v 6 says, that the Lord is a rewarder of those who diligently seek Him. I reasoned that the Lord would know I was only coming to Him for the "reward," but I figured that He set the terms, and I would be ok to seek Him for this reason.

I began a quest. I set aside every day at 10 A.M. to not answer any phone calls, and to go upstairs to Paul's study to worship and read my Bible. I did this every day for many weeks. I was beginning to really enjoy this time with the Lord. I talked to Him about needing the money for the trip, but that wasn't all I talked about to Him. A neighbor down our street, invited me for coffee one morning. She was a friend that I was wanting to lead to the Lord. I agreed to go to her house for coffee, but the feeling of missing my 10 A.M. time with the Lord, strangely bothered me. After our visit was over, I literally ran up the hill to our house with Priscilla in her stroller, and into Paul's study, we went. It felt like a race to get back to my time with God, and I was excited to reconnect with Him. Priscilla was always content, no matter what I was doing. She was happy to play or sleep while I was praying. On this day, I was having the best time ever with the Lord. I remember realizing that nothing had changed financially. It didn't seem to matter. I told the Lord that I loved Him so much. If he was to give us the money for the trip, and it meant that I wouldn't need to seek Him like I was doing, then I'd rather have this closeness than the trip. At that moment, my relationship with Jesus, meant far more than any trip.

The very next morning when our mail was delivered, there was a letter from Dave Soleim. In that letter, was a check for two thousand dollars!! Dave explained that he had written the check weeks ago and put it in his desk drawer to mail us. But the check had found its way to the back of the drawer. He was cleaning out his drawer when he found it and mailed it right away. The timing of this will always be precious to me.

In July of 1978, Paul and I arrived at LAX. Dave and Jackie were there to meet us. They wanted to take us to a restaurant as our first experience in America. As we drove in their car, I noticed the American flags. There seemed to be one on almost every building. This was new to both of us. In New Zealand, we didn't see any flags at all. The schools I taught at, had no flags, and neither were there flags on any buildings. The look of the flags, made us feel happy. Jackie explained that America was very patriotic. Once seated at the restaurant, we noticed several people were openly giving thanks for their food before eating. This was really something we weren't used to seeing. It felt different here. We loved it. It was a small, but powerful moment that made us feel like we were exactly where we were supposed to be.

Dave and Jackie drove us to the hotel we were going to stay at with them. The hotel was close to the Anaheim Convention Center where the meetings were to be held. The hotel was full of people everywhere, all staying for the convention. Some people came up to us to try to sell us things from various pyramid companies. Jackie explained that this was normal in America for sales opportunities. Dave and Jackie knew so many people there. They introduced us to many of their friends, who were very welcoming.

The convention meetings were so incredible. The atmosphere, music, speakers, and even the crowding of so many people seemed wonderful. One of the speakers, was a charismatic Catholic priest. He was outstanding to listen to. Outside in the streets, everything looked bigger. The roads were wider, the cars seemed more modern,, and the atmosphere seemed free.

When the convention was over, I told Dave and Jackie, that I felt like God lived in America. Before we started on our drive up to Seattle with the Soleims, we went to a nearby restaurant for lunch. While eating at our table together, a man came up to our table, who had been at the convention. The man introduced himself, and said that as he was at his table, the Lord had caused him to notice Paul and me, and that he wanted to tell us some things from the Lord. Dave and Jackie agreed to come back to our hotel room with us, to talk to this man. Without telling the man anything, he proceeded to tell us exactly what was going on in our church back in New Zealand. The way the control worked, the cramped feeling of fear of leaving the church, and other things he could not have known without this being a Word of Knowledge from the Lord. Dave and Jackie knew this man was accurate, because we had told them all about things pertaining to our church and culture. Paul and I decided that when we returned to New Zealand, we would leave our church. The man had said that he "saw" us moving north". To us, that meant looking for a church further north in our city. We had no idea that God had other ideas about moving north. God thinks big!

Our road trip back to Seattle to Dave and Jackie's home, was an amazing adventure. We stayed at various hotels along the way and visited many places. Carmel, Monterey, Fisherman's Wharf, San Francisco, Redding, and many other scenic places. All the hotels we stayed at, seemed luxurious, and every building had an American flag on it. The flags were everywhere, and they made everything feel so grand and patriotic. Our conversations with the Soleims were intense, spiritual, and personal. Once in Seattle at the Soleim's home, we met their family of five children. Somehow, Jackie made room for us to stay with their family. We went to their church with them, and again, we experienced that atmosphere of freedom, openness, and a sense of something we couldn't name. However, we knew that whatever it was, we didn't have that special feeling back in New Zealand. The time came very quickly for us to leave Dave and Jackie in Seattle, and move on to Tulsa. This would be the last leg of our journey, before returning home to New Zealand. Paul and I were on our own now, and very grateful for our introduction to American culture at the time. Dave Soleim had arranged for a friend of his, who was going to Camp meeting, to meet us at the Tulsa airport at 3 p.m. We felt a little nervous about the transition, but we were eager for the next chapter of our adventure. This was a mistake, as our flight was to arrive at 1 p.m. However, due to delays with flights, and Paul and I being disoriented at baggage claim, we ended up arriving at Tulsa airport at 3 p.m. We did not have cell phones back then, so we looked for Dave's friend by the description he had given us. Bob and his wife, Sandy, picked us out of the crowd, and took us to our Williams Plaza Hotel, where they were also staying. The meetings were to begin the next morning.

Paul and I were so excited to go to our first-morning meeting. The Cox Convention Center was a very large building. As we walked in, the first thing we noticed, was a huge banner, spread from one side of the stage area to the other. The words on the banner said, "Teach My People Faith". We knew we were going to have a great time. Ushers came up to us to take us to our seats. When the usher knew that we had come from New Zealand, he escorted us to the first floor, right next to the stage. This was labelled, "Foreign Section". We had never thought of ourselves as "foreign", and it sounded strange. But in America, we were foreign. These were the best seats in the building, reserved for people coming in from other countries. After the opening ceremonies, the music began. The music was outstanding. Most of the music was led by Len Mink, with a few solos. The spirit of God was easily felt in the building. The first speaker was Dr. Fred Price. Each speaker brought so much faith teaching that filled us with knowledge in detail that we had not been taught. We took notes at every meeting. The evening meeting was a highlight. Kenneth Hagin Senior was the speaker. Singers included, David Ingles, Rick McKnight, and Len Mink. As the week went on, there were many great speakers. Each of the speakers was powerful and taught Faith in their own unique way. Speakers included, Charles Capps, Norvel Hayes, several others, and our favorite, John Osteen.

One evening, prior to the meeting, Paul and I decided to go to where the speakers' books were being sold downstairs. As we got there, we saw John Osteen setting up his table with the books he had written. We were early and there were not many people around. I decided to go and talk to him. John Osteen welcomed my approach. I told him my whole story about Leukemia, from start to finish. As I spoke to him, he raised his hands to God, with tears running down his face, and said. "You have no idea how difficult it was for me to write that book. It had many interruptions. I told the Lord that if it only helps one person, even if they live on the other side of the world, it will be worth it." That meeting, was a wonderful encounter.

Finally, the Camp meeting was over. Our notebooks were full of valuable things learned, and now we had to prepare to return to New Zealand. Our trip to America was over.

CHAPTER 9.

PREPARING TO MOVE ON

Once back home, there was a settling-in period. We continued our letters and occasional phone calls to Dave and Jackie in Seattle. We were asked to speak about our trip to our church. However, this brought jealousy and many problems with our pastor, who didn't like our love for the word of faith. I felt waves of fear go through me when Paul told the pastor that we were leaving. He narrowed his eyes as he looked at Paul and said, "Leaving won't do anything for you, and you won't amount to anything." We left our church and found another one further into the city. We discussed this with Dave Soleim, and he told us that he had been thinking about an idea to bring us to America. Dave owned several businesses, and his idea was that Paul could work for him in sales for one of his businesses. Dave was prepared to do all the paperwork to sponsor us. This was very exciting for Paul and me, but there was much to consider with a family of four children. The more we thought about going to America, the more involved we became. We discussed it every day, and we wanted our children to experience what we had felt in America.

Dave was becoming very involved with the legalities of sponsoring us. Every time the phone rang, we rushed to answer it. My mother and other relatives were against the whole idea. They told us every negative thing they could think of to discourage us. "What if things don't work out?" "What if you struggle?" "What if it's a mistake?" They planted doubts in our minds, but instead of stopping us, their negativity only made us more determined. We felt trapped in our current situation, and every reason they gave us to stay only reminded us of how much we wanted to leave.

Finally, Dave called with the news we had dreaded. He told us that the government had ruled that the sales position he wanted to offer Paul had to be advertised to Americans first. Since many people would qualify, we knew this meant the opportunity was lost. There was no point in hoping anymore.

We were all deeply disappointed. It felt like a death—a death of a vision. The bottom dropped out of our dream, and it took time to recover from the shock.

Months passed. Life moved on, but the longing for something more never faded.

One day, as I was looking through some of Paul's army documents, something caught my eye. I saw his middle name, "Stevens," and for the first time, I really paid attention to it. Why is there an 's' at the end? I thought. It didn't seem right. I asked Paul if he had ever noticed it before, but he hadn't given it much thought either.

We both agreed that the name seemed misspelled. Paul suggested we send away for a copy of his birth certificate to check. This meant writing to Toronto, Canada, to the Registry of Births, Deaths, and Marriages. In 1978, things were different—no cell phones, no computers. Finding information wasn't as easy as a quick online search. Paul had to go to the public library to get the correct address.

When the birth certificate finally arrived, it felt like receiving a special gift. The envelope was beautifully designed, with a gold crest and Canadian stamps. It felt important. It felt different.

As we opened it, something clicked. The name "Stevens" wasn't a mistake—it was Paul's mother's maiden name! Suddenly, we weren't just holding a birth certificate. We were holding a new possibility.

Paul was born in Toronto, Canada, and when he was six months old, his family moved to Vancouver, British Columbia. After three years there, they left for New Zealand on a ship called *The Marine Phoenix*. Eventually, they settled in Dunedin, in the South Island, where Paul grew up.

Since both Paul and I had spent our lives in Dunedin, Canada felt like a distant land, a place that had never really meant anything to us. But the gold crest on the envelope kept pulling at our curiosity.

We started looking at maps, reading about Canada, and trying to understand the culture. Whenever we met people with a North American accent, we would ask, "Are you from America?" More often than not, the answer was, "No, Canada."

We talked about our growing curiosity with Dave. After many discussions, he suggested we consider British Columbia, since it was close to Washington. But Paul and I didn't want Canada to be a backdoor route to America. If we were going to move, it had to be because we were genuinely excited about Canada—not because we still secretly wished for America.

The problem was, we knew no one there. We had no connections, no job offers, no guarantees. It was just a distant place on a map, and yet, something about it felt right.

We couldn't make such a big decision lightly, especially with four young children under ten years old. We needed more than just excitement—we needed certainty.

Paul and I had a strong relationship. We talked about everything, and even when we disagreed, we worked through it. This decision would be no different. We decided to seek guidance from God.

Paul made a commitment: every day during his lunch break, he would go to an open church near his workplace and pray. We called it "getting it in writing"—our way of saying we wanted clear direction, not just vague feelings.

Each evening, when Paul came home, I would ask, "Did you get anything today?" Some days, he felt hopeful. Other days, he felt nothing. But he kept going, every single day, for four weeks.

Then one evening, we talked about the nature of his prayers.

"Am I just repeating myself?" Paul wondered. "Is God getting tired of hearing the same thing?"

So the next day, he decided to do something different. Instead of praying about our move, he chose to pray for the Prime Minister of Canada, who at the time was Joe Clark.

The next day, Paul went to the church during his lunch hour as usual. It had become a daily ritual—one that gave him peace, even when there were no clear answers. That day, he had a great time in prayer, feeling a deep sense of connection and trust.

As he stood up to leave, something unexpected happened.

The Bible, which had been resting on the chair beside him, suddenly fell open on its own. Paul glanced down, and his eyes were immediately drawn to a verse:

Ezekiel 36:11 (RSV)

"And I will multiply upon you man and beast; and they shall increase and be fruitful; and I will establish you as at your early beginning, and will do more good to you than ever before. Then you will know that I am the Lord."

Paul's heart pounded. This wasn't just coincidence—it felt like an answer. A direct message. A promise.

He read the words over and over. The verse spoke of increase, fruitfulness, new beginnings, and blessings greater than before. It felt personal, as if God was telling him, *Go. Step into something new. I will take care of you.*

When Paul came home that evening, I didn't even have to ask. One look at his face, and I knew.

His eyes were bright, his whole posture different. He had received what he was searching for.

"What happened?" I asked, excited but already knowing the answer.

Paul sat down and told me about the Bible falling open and the verse that had leaped out at him. It was exactly what we needed—a clear confirmation.

For months, we had wrestled with uncertainty. We had waited, searched, and prayed for direction. Now, we had it..

We were going to Canada.

Excitement filled our home. There was so much to do, so many preparations to make. It wouldn't be easy, but now we had a deep sense of peace.

The next chapter of our lives was about to begin.

And this time, nothing could stop us.

CHAPTER 10.

PREPARING FOR CANADA

The first thing we did was apply for passports for Paul and the children. I would need landed immigrant status, but Paul had no problem. The children could receive passports by descent through their father, as long as they were not over two years of age. The only child who qualified was Priscilla. We contacted Canadian Internal Affairs, who told us that our three older children could have a delayed application, as long as we could prove they were all from the same parents. That was easy with a copy of our marriage certificate. However, I was required to write a statement explaining why I wanted all the children to be Canadian. This essentially became an essay about why family unity was so important to us.

Since I was the only one needing landed immigrant status, the Canadian government strongly advised us not to sell our house until I had been approved. Once approved, we would have six months to check into a Canadian port of entry, or the approval would become invalid. Getting approved for immigrant status was no small task. The paperwork was intense, and finding the right answers to all the questions was equally challenging. The immigration department wanted to know everything about me—from past surgeries and medical history to any organizations I had been involved with, traffic tickets I had received, jobs I had held, and every level of education I had completed. I even had to undergo an x-ray to ensure I wasn't bringing an "unborn immigrant" into Canada.

In 1979, no one in New Zealand had cell phones or computers. Everything had to be done through regular mail, which meant every document, form, and request took weeks, if not months, to process. Paul spent countless hours at the library, searching for job listings in the *Vancouver Sun* newspaper. He was qualified in accounting, building science, and quantity surveying, but none of the available positions seemed right for him. We knew moving without a job would be difficult, but at that point, we had decided to trust the process and take things one step at a time.

It is worth mentioning here that one morning during my devotional time, I read a verse I had never noticed before— Psalm 32:6: "For this cause everyone who is godly shall pray to You in a time when You may be found; Surely in a flood of great waters, they shall not come near him." At the time, I didn't think much of it. After all, we lived on HighCliff Road, which was at least seven hundred feet above sea level. However, because the verse specifically said "everyone," I decided to include it in my prayers anyway. I didn't know it at the time, but this verse would later take on a much deeper meaning.

Finally, in January 1980, my immigration status was approved. This gave us until June of that year to arrive in Canada. Our next step was selling our house, but that proved to be another challenge. In New Zealand at the time, real estate agents had exclusive rights to properties, and there was no multiple listing system. Even though it was summertime, the housing market was at an all-time low. There were interested buyers, but most wanted to purchase on a contingency basis—something we were hesitant to accept, as it was too risky.

By March, with no offers coming through, we reconsidered and decided that any offer, even if contingent, would now be considered. In mid-March, a contingency offer finally came in. We had wonderful friends who prayed for us, and within another week, the buyers managed to sell their own house. By early April, our house sale was complete. The pressure was on. We were finally making real progress toward our move, but with just a few months left, there was still so much to do.

The countdown to Canada had officially begun.

Everything was moving quickly now. The pieces of our plan were falling into place, but it still felt surreal that we were really doing this.

Dave and Jackie Soleim had graciously offered for us to stay with them in Seattle while Paul went ahead to Vancouver to find a job. The plan was for him to settle in first, and then the rest of us would join him once things were in place. Meanwhile, Paul had to give four weeks' notice at the bank where he was working.

Thankfully, we had wonderful friends who went out of their way to help us sell nearly everything we owned. It was strange watching our belongings disappear, piece by piece—things that had been part of our daily lives for years were now going to new homes. Paul also had to arrange the shipping of his construction tools, which was no small task. The shipping company told him it would take six weeks for his tools to arrive at the port in Vancouver. Since we had no address in Vancouver yet, all he could do was keep the shipping company's phone number and trust everything would work out.

In the middle of all this planning, we made a tough decision. We needed every bit of time and money to prepare for Canada, but we also felt that it was important to say goodbye to Paul's parents in Brisbane, Australia. Selling off a small insurance policy gave us the funds to make the trip. It wasn't the practical choice, but it was the right choice.

My uncle, who lived in Wellington, had a brother named Trevor, who pastored a large church in Brisbane. Uncle Noel suggested that while we were there, we should meet Trevor, as he had contacts in Surrey, Vancouver. That connection could be valuable, so we made sure to follow up.

When we arrived in Brisbane, our visit with Paul's parents and sister was brief but meaningful. I contacted Trevor, and he invited us to his church service the next day. I was honored when he asked me to sing, something I often did in Dunedin. After church, Trevor invited us to his home to discuss our plans for Canada.

Trevor was incredibly kind and told us about a large church in Surrey, Vancouver, where he often did exchange preaching. He immediately reached out to the Canadian pastor and explained our situation. To our amazement, the pastor arranged for us to stay in the student campus accommodations on the church grounds. Not only that, but we could have our meals in the student kitchen while the students were away on summer break. It was an incredible answer to prayer—something we could never have arranged on our own.

We were also given the pastor's phone number in case we needed any help. This was a huge relief. We weren't just heading into the unknown anymore—there were people waiting to welcome us. Though our trip to Brisbane was short, it was worth every moment.

Back in Dunedin, things became a whirlwind of final preparations. It felt like every day was packed with tasks—selling furniture, closing accounts, making arrangements, and saying goodbye. Paul's best friend, Ron, who lived in Oamaru, came to visit. The two of them had a long history of friendship, and Ron worked full-time for Youth for Christ, traveling across New Zealand.

That night in our kitchen, Ron talked to us about the story of the Israelites leaving Egypt for the Promised Land. He saw a similarity between their journey and ours. As he prayed for us, he suddenly paused and said, "I feel that when you leave on your trip, God is going to give you a gift—just like when the children of Israel left Egypt with gifts."

We had no idea what that meant, but we tucked his words into our hearts. There was something special about the way he said it, and we wouldn't forget it.

A few days later, we received a letter from Jackie. She asked, "How goes the exodus of the Beveridges?" Her words made me think back to the story of the Israelites again. That simple question led me to re-read the Exodus story, and one detail stood out: they left at night.

I was the one in charge of booking plane tickets, and I knew it was time to finalize our flights. My mother, naturally heartbroken that we were leaving, had one request—she begged me not to fly on Pan American Airlines. A crash involving that airline had recently killed several people in our neighborhood, and she was terrified.

I wasn't moved by this fear, but something about the timing of our departure stuck with me. If the Israelites left at night, maybe we should too.

We planned to leave Dunedin and fly to Auckland, where we would spend one last night with my brother. My mother would fly up with us to say goodbye. When I went to book our flights from Auckland to Seattle, I found three options: Air New Zealand, United, and Pan American.

Although both Air New Zealand and United left in the evening, it was still light outside until after 9 p.m. in May. The only flight that truly left at night was Pan American—at 11 p.m.

And so, despite my mother's fears, that's the flight we chose.

Everything was set. We had our tickets, our plan, and a place to stay in Vancouver. There was no turning back now.

Canada was waiting.

CHAPTER 11.

OUR EXODUS!

Of course, Snoopy would be coming with us. The authorities stated that he had to be transported in an aluminum crate, custom-made to fit his size, along with the necessary paperwork. We arranged for him to stay at an excellent kennel a few days before our departure on May 10th. The thought of leaving him behind, even temporarily, was difficult, but we knew this was the best way to ensure his safety.

Since we needed the kennel crate made quickly, we were fortunate to know someone who could build it for us on short notice. Snoopy had to remain at the kennel indefinitely until we received confirmation of when we could pick him up in Vancouver. We had no idea how long it would take—maybe a few days or even weeks—but we trusted the process. The owner of the kennel was amazing—kind, understanding, and completely reassuring. We estimated it could be up to three weeks before Snoopy could join us, so we arranged suitable payment with the kennel owner, who agreed to personally take him to the airport once we provided the confirmed date. Knowing Snoopy was in good hands made parting a little easier.

Finally, the long-anticipated day arrived. Our goodbyes had been said, and we all felt at peace, knowing we were following God's plan. We locked the house door and, with hearts racing, moved excitedly toward our friends' cars, which were waiting on the street to take us to the airport. We didn't look back—this was the beginning of a brand-new chapter.

The flight from Dunedin to Auckland was smooth, and upon arrival, my brother David picked us up and took us to his home. My mother was with us, and although she tried to hide it, she was quietly upset. This transition was hard for her too, but she supported us wholeheartedly. That evening, David had arranged a farewell high tea with several friends he had invited. The gathering was warm and heartfelt, and as the evening went on, people slowly began to leave.

As the house quieted down, I found myself alone in a side room, lost in thought about the journey that awaited us the next day. Excitement and nerves intertwined as I mentally prepared for the big move. One of David's guests, Don Dickson—who both Paul and I knew—entered the room. At the time, Don was ministering in Auckland. It was just the two of us in the room when he spoke to me.

"Delwyn," he said, "I know you're excited about your trip tomorrow. But things sometimes go wrong with overseas travel. What would you do if, when you arrive at the airport, the airline tells you that you can't board the plane due to some unexpected issue?"

I silently thought to myself, "He has no idea how sure we are about this journey." Confidently, I responded with a verse from Romans 8:28. "Well, Don, if that happened, I would say, 'This will work for our good.'"

Don simply nodded. "Well, good. I hope it all works out." And with that, he turned and left the room.

The next day—the big day—had finally arrived. We packed all our cases into the car and made the drive to the airport. The reality of what we were doing hit harder with each passing mile.

As we arrived, Sarah suddenly said she felt sick. Perhaps it was nerves, or maybe exhaustion from the emotional farewells. Paul headed to the Pan American counter with my brother and mother, who were helping with the children, while I walked further along to the ticket counter to present our tickets.

Strangely, I was the only one at the counter. For a moment, I wondered if we were too early. Then, a man in a smart uniform approached, looked over our tickets, and spoke.

"Beveridge? Family of six?"

"Yes," I replied, my heart pounding slightly.

The man continued. "I'm sorry, but I have some bad news for you. You won't be able to fly out tonight because there's been a change."

I was stunned. For a few seconds, I could only stare at him, unable to process his words. This wasn't supposed to happen. We were ready. Everything had been planned.

The man studied my expression and then asked, "What do you have to say about that?"

In that instant, Don's words from the night before replayed in my mind—almost as if they had been preparing me for this exact moment. Without hesitation, I responded, "Well, this will work for our good."

The man smiled. "That's great. Now get your husband and head over to that office. Someone will be there to speak with you."

I turned and called out, "Paul! Dear, we can't go tonight. We have to go to that office over there."

The moment Sarah heard this, she promptly threw up—right there, on the floor by the counter. It was as if her body had reacted before her mind could process the disappointment.

Thankfully, my mother quickly stepped in to care for the children, while Paul and I headed toward the office. Uncertainty loomed over us, but deep inside, I held onto the belief that somehow, in some way, this was all part of the plan.

This was no ordinary office. It was lavish and sophisticated, with plush red velvet chairs arranged neatly for visitors. The atmosphere felt surreal, as if we had suddenly stepped into a world far removed from the airport chaos outside.

A Pan-American officer in uniform entered and greeted us with a calm, professional demeanor. He invited us to sit down and then, with a serious expression, began to speak.

"I want to personally apologize," he said. "The flight is overcrowded, and unfortunately, we need your seats."

It felt like a punch to the gut. We sat there in stunned silence, unable to respond. Everything had been planned so carefully, and now, at the last moment, everything was changing.

Our silence must have unsettled the officer because he quickly continued, trying to soften the blow.

"Of course, we here at Pan-American will compensate you for this inconvenience. We will issue you a check for $2,400, put your entire family up at the Ritz Hotel for the night, and provide you with tickets for dinner and a show."

He paused, watching our faces for a reaction. We were still too shocked to speak.

Then he added, "Additionally, we will fly you out tomorrow night in business class and notify the party that is expecting you. Will this be acceptable to you?"

We barely processed the words before quietly nodding in agreement. The officer then escorted us to another area where Paul was handed the check, along with our new tickets and arrangements for a limousine to take us to the hotel and back to the airport the next day.

The children, far from disappointed, were thrilled about an unexpected night at the Ritz Hotel and an exciting show.

For them, this felt more like an adventure than a setback. My mother was equally delighted—an extra day with us was a blessing she hadn't expected.

Later that evening, as Paul and I reflected on everything, we remembered Ron's prayer in our kitchen before we left. He had prayed that our journey would resemble the exodus of the Israelites—who left Egypt with unexpected gifts. And here we were, receiving an unexpected blessing, just as he had prayed! Truly, God is good.

When we arrived in Seattle, a wave of relief washed over us. We were greeted by our dear friends, the Soleims, who had gone out of their way to make us feel welcome. They even moved out of their master bedroom so we could stay comfortably in their home. Their kindness was overwhelming, and we were incredibly grateful.

Just two days later, Paul made arrangements by phone to fly to Vancouver ahead of us. Our new life was beginning, and the pieces were starting to fall into place. The pastor of the church we were to be associated with had arranged for someone to pick Paul up from the airport and take him to the student housing. It was a humble but welcoming place, run by an elderly couple, Mr. and Mrs. Banning, who lovingly maintained the accommodations. They were absolutely delighted to have Paul there.

Meanwhile, I was missing Paul terribly. The uncertainty of everything was difficult, but we held onto our faith that things would work out. After a week without securing a job, Paul called and said it was time for the rest of us to join him in Vancouver. We decided to move forward together, trusting that we would find our way.

Paul, tired of navigating the new city by bus, had purchased an old but reliable station wagon. It wasn't fancy, but it would be our means of getting around in this unfamiliar place. Dave, ever supportive, drove the children and me to the airport, where we prayed together for our future before we departed.

When we arrived in Vancouver, Paul was there waiting for us at the airport. The moment we saw him, all the uncertainty seemed to fade. I checked in with immigration just in time, making my deadline by June—yet another amazing fulfillment of what we had hoped for.

Paul had done remarkably well finding his way around, especially considering there was no GPS back then. He relied entirely on a directory of maps, which he carried with him at all times. It was a challenge, especially since he had to adjust to driving on the opposite side of the road compared to New Zealand.

At the student quarters, we received a warm welcome from Mr. and Mrs. Banning. Their hospitality was a great comfort in this new chapter of our lives. To our delight, they had no objections to us bringing Snoopy to live with us there. Hearing this felt like the final missing piece falling into place.

Paul immediately called the kennel where Snoopy was staying and arranged for him to be flown out the next day. The kennel owner, experienced with such arrangements, knew exactly what to do and soon phoned us back with the flight itinerary.

Two days later, we made our way to the airport's animal holding area to pick up Snoopy. We could hardly contain our excitement—we had missed him so much and hoped he would be just as happy to see us.

However, finding the exact location where he had been moved was not easy. We wandered around, asking for directions, growing more anxious with each passing minute. Finally, we spotted his aluminum crate, which had large holes in the sides. At first, we were confused—then we realized what had happened. Snoopy had desperately tried to chew his way out.

Then we heard it—the unmistakable sound of his tail thumping against the crate.

He knew we were there.

The moment we spoke, he erupted into excited whimpers and frantic wagging. We quickly opened the crate, ready to comfort him. But as we did, we noticed something strange. His teeth—his once white, strong teeth—were now covered in aluminum.

Snoopy had literally bitten his way through the metal, trying to get to us.

Despite his ordeal, he was overjoyed to be reunited with us. The student quarters may not have been luxurious, but to Snoopy, it was home, because we were there.

With everything coming together, Paul took the Pan-American check to a bank in Vancouver. To our amazement, after converting it into Canadian dollars, the amount was more than enough to completely cover all our travel expenses—including every single charge for Snoopy.

Looking back, we realized that what had seemed like an inconvenience at the airport had actually been a blessing in disguise.

God had provided for us in ways we never could have imagined.

Time was racing by, and Paul urgently needed to find a job. Each passing day brought a mix of faith and anxiety, but we chose to focus on trust. We changed the way we prayed about it—instead of asking, we began thanking God in advance for providing the right opportunity. We knew that He would come through for us.

Meanwhile, we had started attending the church that had so graciously accommodated us. It quickly became more than just a place of worship—it became a community. We made new friends, and one of them, Gary, turned out to be instrumental in what was about to happen.

One evening, Gary came to visit us at the student quarters. It was a casual visit, just a friendly chat, but it would soon turn into something far more significant. Paul had shared with him the kind of job he was looking for—something related to construction, specifically in concrete forming and quantity surveying.

Gary listened and then, almost offhandedly, mentioned something incredible.

"You know," he said, "I was recently offered a construction manager position, but I turned it down because I'm happy where I am. But it sounds like it could be a perfect fit for you, Paul."

Our ears perked up instantly.

Gary went on to explain that the position was with *Sky-Hi Scaffolding Ltd.*, and he had all the contact details. Without hesitation, Paul followed up on it. It all happened so fast— like a divine setup. Before we knew it, the owner of *Sky-Hi Scaffolding*, James Johnson, had called and requested an interview—with both of us.

The day of the interview felt significant. There was an unshakable feeling that this was the opportunity we had been waiting for.

Paul and I drove to James Johnson's beautiful home, a stunning property that exuded success. I remember watching Paul navigate the drive confidently—despite the challenge of switching from New Zealand's right-hand driving system to Canada's left-hand steering and right-side road rules. He had adapted so quickly, and I was proud of him.

When we arrived, we received a warm and friendly welcome. James was hospitable and professional, putting us at ease right away. He had prepared refreshments for us, and after some casual conversation, he and Paul got down to business.

James brought out a massive construction blueprint—a detailed plan for a commercial building. I remember the sheer size of it, covering nearly the entire table.

"Take your time," James said. "Look over it and let me know if you think you can handle taking off the quantities and pricing everything accordingly."

Paul leaned over the table, studying the plan carefully. I stood beside him, watching as he analyzed the details. Then, I heard him murmur softly, almost to himself—

"It's all in metric."

A moment of hesitation flickered in his eyes.

Paul had been working in banking for the past few years, and he hadn't needed to use the metric system in construction during that time. It was a challenge—but I knew Paul. He wasn't one to back down.

He looked up and, with unwavering confidence, said, "I can do anything when I put my mind to it."

James liked that. He saw in Paul not just experience, but determination and a problem-solving attitude.

"I like your background," James said, nodding approvingly. "And I really like your attitude. If you want the job, it's yours!"

We could hardly believe it.

This was far beyond what we had expected—a managerial position, exactly in Paul's field, and offered to him on the spot!

But the blessings didn't stop there.

The job came with a brand-new, modern company car! That very night, Paul drove it home, while I followed behind in our family car. It was a surreal moment—just days ago, we were praying for provision, and now we were driving home with a new car and a job offer in hand!

The very next day, Paul started work at the *Sky-Hi* office. God's faithfulness was undeniable.

Looking back, we could see how every little detail had been orchestrated—from meeting Gary at church, to the perfect timing of the job opportunity, to Paul's willingness to step out in faith despite the challenges.

This was more than just a job. It was confirmation that we were exactly where we were meant to be.

CHAPTER 12.

LIFE IN CANADA!

We were now in a position to look for a home to buy. The students were due back in our campus accommodations in four weeks, so we definitely had no time to waste. Paul contacted a realtor whose name and number had been given to us by a new friend from the church. It felt reassuring to have a recommendation from someone we trusted. We knew we wanted to live close to the Washington border so we could visit the Soleims frequently.

The realtor showed us houses in Langley, where we found a beautiful home located in a quiet cul-de-sac close to schools. It had four bedrooms and was already empty, making it ideal for a quick move-in. The owners were eager to sell and assured us that we could move in as soon as the loan was approved. Fortunately, the approval came through just in time, giving us a full week to move before we had to vacate our campus accommodations.

Paul kept calling the number he had been given to arrange the pickup of our belongings from the ship. We knew international shipping could take time, but the wait felt longer than expected. Thankfully, everything arrived that week. Using the maps Paul had become quite skilled at navigating, we were able to locate the shipping warehouse and collect our things. I could hardly wait to set up our new home.

We had been given contacts for furniture stores and other essential places, making it easier to furnish the house. Our street, 196th, had about twenty houses, and it didn't take long for us to meet some of our neighbors. One kind neighbor even helped us set up utility connections and guided us through other important tasks. I still remember the joy I felt when the phone rang for the first time. The sound was so comforting, a small but powerful reminder of stability and home. I couldn't wait to answer it. It was a call from Sears, informing us that our furniture delivery was scheduled. This was a big moment—it meant our new life was taking shape.

It was August 1980, and we soon realized that the children needed to be enrolled in school. Thankfully, the schools were close by, and the enrollment process was simple. Daniel was placed directly into a French immersion program, where every subject was taught in French. At first, we wondered how he would adjust, but to our surprise, he picked up the language incredibly fast.

We also found a large Charismatic church in the area, which had excellent programs for families. I became actively involved in a weekly ladies' Bible study group, where I met some wonderful women who soon became close friends. Before long, we started hosting a small group meeting in our home every week. These gatherings were uplifting and life-changing, deepening our connections within the community. Eventually, Paul and I were invited to teach classes on marriage and family issues at the church.

I led one of the ladies' Bible study groups, while Paul became involved with the Langley chapter of Full Gospel Businessmen. It felt like we were exactly where we were meant to be. Both of us were often asked to speak at various local church groups, and we embraced these opportunities with gratitude.

On the home front, Paul kept busy with projects around the house. He built an extra bedroom and even constructed a dollhouse in the backyard for our two younger daughters. Seeing their excitement made all his hard work worthwhile. We also put up a fence around the property, giving Snoopy, our dog, the freedom to run outside safely. Life was settling in well—Paul loved his job, the children were happy at school, and we had just purchased our very first television set.

Across the street and down a few houses lived a retired Women's Army Corps lady named Marg Hagman. Marg adored our children and often stopped by to chat or offer to babysit when needed. One time, when one of our children had to stay at Vancouver Children's Hospital for a short period, Marg stepped in without hesitation. She picked up the other children from school, fed them dinner, and stayed with them until we returned in the evening. Her kindness and generosity were an incredible blessing to us.

Around this time, we began listening to a radio program hosted by a pastor from a church just across the Washington border in Lynden. His teachings resonated deeply with us, reminding us of the inspiring lessons we had heard during our visit to Tulsa in 1978. For an entire year, we faithfully tuned in to his messages, feeling drawn to his church even before we knew exactly where it was. Eventually, we decided to visit one Sunday—and little did we know, this decision would play a significant role in our journey later on.

In 1982, Daniel turned twelve years old. He had benefited greatly from being in the French immersion program and was smarter than most kids his age. His ability to pick up languages so quickly amazed us. He expressed a desire to learn to play the guitar. We saw an advertisement on television about a guitar sale in Vancouver and decided to take the whole family along for the trip. It felt like a fun adventure.

It was a Saturday in February. It had been raining for a few days, and the air smelled fresh and damp. But the family outing to buy a guitar was too exciting to stay home. We bought the guitar and headed home to Langley, in the Brookswood area.

As we neared our street, we saw police cars and other official-looking men telling us to stop. Something was clearly wrong. It looked like floodwaters had taken over the whole intersection. We asked what had happened and were told that a mysterious flood had occurred on our street and the surrounding streets, and we were not allowed to enter unless our home was there. The police said that they were investigating. Our hearts pounded as we waited to hear more.

When we gave them our address, we were allowed to drive very slowly to our home. The sight ahead was both shocking and unsettling. The water everywhere was very concerning. It had spread across the neighborhood like an uninvited guest. Since we had left our house to go to

Vancouver, we could now see that the houses on our street had water covering their front lawns, creeping up their driveways.

Our driveway had about three feet of water at the front, extending back into the street at about six inches deep. Our driveway had a very gentle rise in it, but it looked flat. The whole scene felt surreal. This was indeed a mystery, and we wanted to know what had happened.

I was looking out the window from the second story, watching the rain fall even heavier now, when a scripture came into my mind. It was that unusual verse from Psalm 32:6 (NKJV):

"For this cause everyone who is godly shall pray to You in a time when You may be found; Surely in a flood of great waters, they shall not come near him."

I had prayed this very verse in New Zealand before we came to Canada and had only thought of it occasionally since our move. But now, standing here with floodwaters surrounding us, it suddenly felt more relevant than ever.

I spoke aloud to the Lord as I looked at the floodwater out of our window. I said, "Lord, this cannot happen to our home. You said that if I prayed about this when there wasn't any flood, these waters would not come near me. This should not be happening. I will take authority over this flood, according to Your word, and forbid it to rise any further up our driveway."

Paul and I were in agreement about this. We had seen God's faithfulness before, and we knew this moment was no different.

Neighbors were calling us about water filling up their basements. Panic was spreading through the street. Our area was built in an elevated basin that used pumps to keep the hydrostatic pressure of the water table under control. Apparently, the pumps had failed, and the deluge of 96.8 millimeters of rain was too much for the water table. This was now causing flooded basements, streets, ditches, and fields, with no sign of the rain stopping anytime soon.

Another neighbor called to ask if we had water in our basement. At that moment, we realized—we hadn't even checked.

Daniel's bedroom was in the basement, and we ran downstairs to look. Our hearts raced as we prepared for the worst. There was a sump drain in the tile floor of the basement. When we looked down at the metal grating of the drain, we could see water sitting just below it.

Other neighbors said that the water was rising through their basement drains and flooding every corner of their homes. We knew that Jesus had taken authority over storms in the Bible and had taught His disciples to do the same. This wasn't just a story to us—it was a principle we believed in. We had the authority of having prayed Psalm 32:6 and knew how the Lord said to put Him in remembrance of His word.

I went to get a dinner plate to put over the drain. It seemed like such a simple action, but in faith, it meant everything. We stood around it and commanded the water to stay down. With firm voices, we spoke to the water in Jesus' name, declaring that it would not enter our basement. Then we turned our focus to the water deepening on the road by our driveway. We believed what we were doing and held onto the scripture, trusting that these floodwaters would not overcome our house.

The rains continued to fall, and the local news was full of the story of the Langley floods. Some streets in our neighborhood were so deep with water that people were evacuating in small boats, paddling through what used to be roads. It was a scene we never imagined witnessing. Sandbag trucks lined both sides of the streets, and on every corner, people were working tirelessly to build barriers against the rising water. Men and women, young and old, wore wading pants and rubber boots as they shoveled and stacked sandbags, desperately trying to protect their homes.

Because we believed that the Lord would take care of our house, Paul and I felt peace in our hearts. We left the children at home and went out to help with sandbagging, assisting our struggling neighbors as they fought to save their properties.

When we returned home, we went to check under the plate on the drain in our basement. The water was slightly higher now—right at the edge of the drain. But we refused to let fear take hold. We didn't let what we saw change what we believed. We continued standing on the promise of the scripture and reminded the water that it had no permission to overflow into our house.

Our neighbors on either side of us lost entire bookshelves full of precious collections in their basements. Water-damaged carpets had to be torn out, septic fields were flooded with sewage, and the clean-up was overwhelming. Each time we checked under the plate, the water was right there, pressing against the barrier—but it never rose any higher. It never broke through.

Although the floodwaters continued to rise elsewhere for several days, our house remained completely dry.

This is the beauty of having a real relationship with God. He is not distant—He is present in our lives, responding to faith.

When we came to sell our house in 1986, we discovered something remarkable. The title paper on our house had a blue stamp on it that read:

"Not affected by the flood."

The Bible says that those who bless others will be blessed by God. And in an incredible testimony to that promise, we later found out that Marg Hagman—our dear neighbor who had stood by us in a time of real stress when our daughter was in the hospital—had the exact same stamp on her property title.

Out of all the homes on our street, ours and Marg's were the only two that were not affected by the flood.

The Vancouver Sun

MONDAY, FEBRUARY 15, 1982   VANCOUVER, BRITISH COLUMBIA   ★★★   25 CENTS

PIGGYBACK . . . Paul Beveridge carries son, Daniel, through heavily flooded area of Langley. (Another picture, A3.)

Another Unexpected Trial – Daniel's Computer

Daniel's guitar-buying day was not the only dramatic moment we had.

Daniel loved his old computer but had outgrown its capabilities. He needed an upgrade and had spent weeks researching the perfect model. He had found exactly what he wanted, and we promised it to him for his birthday.

I found a computer shop in Surrey that was having a sale on the very model Daniel wanted. Excited, I picked up the phone and called the store. The man who answered assured me that they had it in stock, and after I explained that we were on our way, he promised to put one aside for us. I even gave him my name to ensure the reservation was secure.

97

Daniel was beyond excited. He could barely sit still in the car, talking non-stop about his new computer and all the things he planned to do with it.

Once we arrived at the store, Daniel and I eagerly walked inside. Our eyes scanned the shelves, looking for the computer we had been promised. We were the only customers there at the time.

I approached the counter and greeted the salesman. With a bright smile, I reminded him of my earlier phone call.

The man looked embarrassed. He hesitated, avoiding my gaze, and then finally spoke.

"I'm so sorry, ma'am, but I just sold it to someone else. It was the last one left in the sale."

My heart sank. I couldn't believe what I was hearing.

It was useless to remind the man that he had personally assured me he would hold one for us. The damage was done.

I turned to look at Daniel. His expression was a mixture of shock and devastation. He had been so excited, and now, in an instant, all of that had been taken away.

We walked around the store, looking at a few other models. But nothing compared to the one he had set his heart on. I bent down and whispered to him, "Don't worry, Son. We'll get you an even better one somewhere else."

As we made our way toward the exit, I silently reflected on a scripture I had read.

When Jesus sent His disciples out to share the Gospel, He told them what to do if they entered a place that did not receive them. He instructed them to "shake the dust off your feet and move on."

Of course, this computer store wasn't a mission field, but the principle still applied. We didn't have to dwell on this disappointment—we could leave it behind and trust that something better was ahead.

As Daniel and I stepped through the doorway, I paused. Then, in a small but meaningful act, I shook my right foot.

We talked of getting another computer as soon as possible, and Daniel was happy. We reassured him that something better was ahead. The next day, in the newspaper, there were pictures and reports about a computer store that had burnt to the ground the night before. To our shock, it was the very same store Daniel and I had visited.

We looked at each other in disbelief. It was a strange and unsettling realization that the computer store had somehow run out of favor!! However, it wasn't long before we purchased an even better computer than Daniel had originally wanted. His excitement was renewed, and we were amazed at how quickly he mastered everything about it.

Paul and I continued to listen to our favorite radio preacher, whose church was just over the Washington border in Lynden. Finally, we decided to find out where this church was and planned to take the family to visit the next Sunday.

We had been visiting the Soleims every couple of months, so we were used to crossing the American border. Each time, it was the same routine—the guards checked our documents, asked questions, and waved us through. Strangely, even though we saw the same guards every time, they never showed signs of recognition.

One day, as we pulled up to the checkpoint, I smiled and casually said to the guard, "It's a wonder you don't recognize us by now."

He never cracked a smile. Without missing a beat, he continued in his usual monotone voice, "Do you have anything to declare?"

Paul and the children could easily state they were Canadian citizens, but I always had to say that I was a Canadian landed immigrant. This usually resulted in me being asked to go inside the building to show my papers. It had become a tiresome routine, but I always carried my documents, knowing what to expect. They also wanted to see my driver's license to check my address.

When we arrived at the church in Lynden, we were immediately and warmly welcomed. The congregation was friendly, and the pastor and his wife seemed to really like our accents. There was an instant connection.

The service was wonderful, filled with heartfelt worship and an inspiring message. Afterward, we stayed and talked at length with the pastor. He was curious about our story—where we had come from, what led us to his church, and how we had found out about it.

We decided to return the next Sunday, and as time went on, we felt more and more at home. By mid-1983, we made a big decision—we left the Canadian church and officially joined the charismatic church in Lynden.

It was only seven miles from our house in Langley to the church in Lynden. The drive was easy, and the more we got involved, the more we found ourselves making the trip often. I was loving the ladies' Bible study group in Lynden. There was a deep sense of sharing and caring among the women, and I felt truly connected.

On the way back to Canada, the guards on that side were much friendlier—probably because they knew most of us were Canadian. Crossing the border became second nature to us.

Becoming Deeply Involved in Ministry

It wasn't long before I was leading a Bible study during the week, and Paul was involved in several activities for men. As the children found their own places in the church, our trips across the border increased. By the time they were involved in youth programs and other activities, we were crossing the border back and forth up to five times a week!

The people at the church in Lynden grew to love us, and we loved them. Paul and I became increasingly involved in ministry. Our roles expanded, and we found ourselves deeply woven into the life of the church.

We led the adult Bible study on Sunday mornings before the main service and frequently worked with the pastor in important decisions for the church. Our experience and passion for helping marriages led to us being asked to co-lead marriage seminars, something we felt deeply called to.

Although we were used to the border crossings, one part of the process became increasingly frustrating for me. Every time we crossed into the U.S., I had to get out of the car, go inside the building, and present my papers—while Paul and the children stayed parked outside, waiting for me.

After years of this routine, I knew it was time to take the next step. I decided to start the application process with the Canadian Consulate to become a full-fledged Canadian citizen.

I had been a permanent resident for over three years, and now it was time to move on. The application process was extensive—forms upon forms, some of them asking the same questions I had answered when applying for landed immigrant status.

Finally, the day came for me to go to the Canadian Consulate and officially become a Canadian citizen. Paul came with me to witness the ceremony.

I had expected something grand—maybe a meaningful speech or a special acknowledgment of this life-changing decision. Instead, the room was plain and bare, except for a Canadian flag and a few simple chairs.

There was no test, no fanfare, and not even a Bible to put my hand on.

I was unceremoniously asked to raise my right hand and recite the Oath of Citizenship, followed by singing the Canadian national anthem with a group of other people. That was it.

It was all over quickly, and it was time to drive home.

I was grateful, of course. It was a relief to know that our whole family was now fully Canadian. No more unnecessary stops at the border. No more extra paperwork.

But as we drove home, I found myself unexpectedly reflective. My heart was calm, but something inside me still felt unfinished. I began to inwardly evaluate what I had just done and why I still had an unsatisfied feeling.

Once we reached home, we went to check the mailbox—a small metal box attached to the side of the house near the front door.

Inside was a long, thick envelope addressed to me. Curious, I opened it right there before walking inside.

Inside the envelope was a promotional brochure for Marilyn Hickey's next international missionary trip—to Ethiopia.

Marilyn Hickey was an American evangelist whom I supported monthly. Her teachings had been a great encouragement to me over the years, but this was different.

The brochure was designed in the form of a realistic American passport.

I held it in my hand for a moment and just stared at it.

Then, clear as day, the Spirit of God spoke to my heart:

"This is next."

I stood frozen for a moment, absorbing what I had just heard.

When I showed the brochure to Paul, we both stood in silence, overwhelmed by the significance of the moment.

Our eyes filled with tears, because deep down, we both knew the truth.

God had just revealed the next step in our journey.

CHAPTER 13.

THE PROMISED LAND

Our commitment in the church at Lynden continued to grow. Both Paul and I were often teaching groups or preaching in the evening services. Meanwhile, we were also asked to speak at various organizations in Langley and Surrey. When we had these opportunities, we kept our theme on teaching people how to have a close relationship with the Word of God and to believe that He is faithful to do what He says.

We observed that many people seemed to think that because they were American and attended church, that this made them Christian. We saw a great need to teach people how to know the Lord intimately and how to apply the Word of God into their everyday lives.

We had been very involved in the church for three years when the pastor ordained both of us for ministry. Shortly after our ordination, the pastor invited us to a special meeting with himself and the board of directors. At this meeting, the pastor invited us to think about becoming full-time assistant pastors in his church. He wanted us there to continue the work we were already doing and for me to take on the counseling needs of the church. We agreed to pray about this and to have further discussions.

Paul and I knew that we loved this ministry work. However, giving up a stable job and supporting our family of six was a huge issue, especially because this would potentially involve moving to Washington with all the legalities involved.

We knew that Amos 3:3 says, "How can two walk together, except they be in agreement?" One evening after dinner, Paul and I sat across the dining table from each other and began our discussion about going into the ministry. We had so many questions for each other. There were details that necessitated agreement, and where there was none, we had to carry on talking about issues until we were in total agreement on every item in the discussion.

Once we reached this point together, we held hands across the table and prayed. Both of us reached a complete peace to say 'yes' to this proposition. We knew that the Lord would have to order our steps and take care of the details, and it would be wonderful to see how He would do it. This was a huge change to prepare for, but we were ready.

It felt like we were stepping into a whole new chapter of life—scary but exciting at the same time. We reminded each other that when God leads, He also provides. That gave us strength to move forward with faith.

The next morning, I had to go to Lynden to teach the ladies' Bible study. As I approached the border at Lynden, I pulled up as usual beside the brick wall of the building. One of our favorite customs officers was waiting for me. As usual, he showed no sign of recognition and asked me the same question he always asked: "Citizens of what country?"

I answered, "Canada." He hesitated, and I saw him looking over at my passenger seat, where I had my Bible and a notebook. He kept staring at the passenger seat and asked me, "What about that big fellow?"

"What big fellow?" I asked.

He ignored me and walked across the front of my car to the passenger window. I hadn't left him much room between my car and the brick wall. He kept staring into the passenger seat with his hand up to his eyes. I couldn't figure out what was going on.

Finally, he came back around to my window. I asked him, "What was it that you thought you saw?"

"On you go," he said, and gestured for me to move on.

As I drove on a little way over the border, the strangest emotion gripped me. I knew that the border guard had seen an angel in my passenger seat. I began to worship the Lord as I drove to the church. "What amazing confirmation You have given me about our decision. You give me favor and I'm so grateful."

I pondered the fact that it was the border guard who saw the angel, and not me. This way, I couldn't dispute what had happened.

It felt like God was gently but powerfully reminding me: "I am with you. I go before you." That moment gave me courage like nothing else could. I knew then, more than ever, that we were walking directly into God's purpose.

Once we told the pastor that we had accepted his offer, he proceeded with an immigration attorney. America allowed churches to request certain specialty staff of immigrant status for employment. The process moved slowly and began with a volley of paperwork to us from the immigration attorney.

Paul had to send copies of sermons he had preached, along with records of various meetings associated with the church. Proof of our counseling involvement hours and many other requirements were needed. This back and forth with necessary forms and items went on for six months.

Finally, we received an invitation for an interview at the American Consulate in Vancouver, in December of 1986. This was green card day for us!! We came to the interview as a family.

An official person came to the waiting room where we were and welcomed us warmly. We were ushered into a cubicle where a man in uniform was behind a counter. He was jovial and very pleasant.

"So you want to be counseling pastors in America, eh? Alright then, let's begin with a demonstration. I'm thinking of getting married and coming to you for counseling. What would you say to me?"

This was home sweet home for us. The question was initially directed to Paul, but we were standing together at this counter. Paul began by asking the man if he and his fiancée were equally yoked.

The man asked, "Well, what do you mean?"

Paul asked him if he and his fiancée were both Christians.

The man replied, "My fiancée is a Christian, but I'm not. Does that make any difference?"

"Yes, it does," Paul replied. "Would you like to become a Christian so that you are both united in your beliefs and faith?"

The man asked us, "Well, how do I do that?"

Together, we began to explain what it meant to be "born again." The man stopped us talking, grinned, and "That's enough!"

Then with that, he stamped our paperwork with deliberate pressure. That was our green card!!

We walked out of that office feeling like we were floating! God had opened a door that no man could shut, and we were filled with joy and awe at how He worked through even a government interview to confirm His plan.

We decided to wait out the school year and made use of the time to plan our move to American permanent residence. In May 1987, Paul gave his notice to Ski-Hi Scaffolding.

Paul had accomplished some really important work in the building industry in Canada. He was construction manager and cost engineer of the Stadium Station for the light rapid transit through Vancouver. Paul would tell me when he came home from work about some of the difficulties he was encountering. There seemed to be so many problems.

Paul told me how one day, he just had to pull off the freeway to a safe area to ask the Lord for help. He opened his Bible, which was always in his car. It opened at Psalm 60:12 (NKJV). The verse he read stood out to him: "Through God, we will do valiantly, for He it is who shall tread down our enemies."

Paul was so relieved. He made a list of all the enemies that were making his job so difficult. The list included the weather, because it rained every day for a month. Other enemies were things like construction machinery problems, various inspectors, and personnel.

Paul was thanking the Lord right there in the car that He would take care of these 'enemies' for him. Once back on the job, Paul met with his four superintendents and told them not to worry anymore about the difficulties, because "God is with us."

The men showed great relief, and after that, things improved until the job was completed.

I remembered the scripture Paul had received which gave us the faith to move to Canada. It was the part about increasing him man and beast and doing more good to him than ever before. Paul was in charge of nineteen men. Later on, we had four pet dogs at our home. Maybe this was the increase in beasts!!

Looking back, it felt like God had been preparing us all along. Every challenge had a purpose. Every answer to prayer was a building block in our journey of faith.

The owner of Ski-Hi was sorry to lose Paul but delighted that his reason for leaving was to become full-time in the ministry. As a parting gift, he gave us two weeks at a lovely timeshare in Maui—all expenses paid!

It was an unexpected blessing. A beautiful way for God to say, "Well done, now rest before your next mission." We were overwhelmed with gratitude.

Before we took the vacation, we were able to rent a house in Lynden and enroll three of the children in schools. Sarah decided to delay going to college so we could stay together as a family and adjust to American life. Sarah began working at a bank. We put our house on the market and celebrated with our vacation in Maui.

Everything was working out well, and God gave us great favor. On our return from Maui, we had an offer on our house, which we accepted. This meant that we could move to Lynden in time for the start of the school year.

It truly felt like every piece was falling into place. God was not only opening doors—we felt like He was walking us through them, hand in hand.

During our time in Lynden, we learned a great deal. Being in the ministry was thrilling, very satisfying, but intense in many other ways. We continued to visit the Soleims regularly, and they reminded us that after five years, we could apply for American citizenship.

The needs of our family were changing. Daniel had graduated from high school with many scholarships and was ready to go to college. During this time, we bought a cockatiel for Jemima, who wanted one very badly. She loved the bird and named him 'Pete.'

Eventually, we taught Pete to say "Praise the Lord," because of a scripture in Psalm 150:6 that says, "Let everything that has breath praise the Lord." Pete was a family favorite, and we all loved him.

He brought so much joy to our home—his cheerful chirping often lifted our spirits, especially during busy or tiring days.

Sarah was longing to complete her college also. After three years of full-time work at the church, we moved to the Greater Seattle area. We prayed as a family about what work Paul would do. It was 1989 when we asked the Lord to open up a way that was right for us all.

The very next evening, Dave Soleim, who knew we were leaving the ministry in Lynden, called us and asked Paul to consider working for him as a controller in his residential construction company, Capstone Homes in Maple Valley.

Close friends from the church in Lynden helped us pack, move, and resettle in our first owned home in America.

It felt like a milestone—owning our first home in a new country. It was a moment full of emotion, gratitude, and hopeful expectation.

One of our friends had Pete in his cage in the trunk of her car. For some reason, she needed to stop suddenly, which caused the bird cage to fall over in her car. I got out of my car to help. After opening the trunk of our friend's car, there was Pete, trying to climb back up onto his perch and chirping loudly, "Praise the Lord."

Even in the chaos of a toppled cage and a bumpy ride, Pete reminded us of a simple but powerful truth: praise isn't just for perfect moments—it's for every moment.

Even a little cockatiel can still give praise when circumstances are not going well.

CHAPTER 14.

LIFE IN AMERICA

After many years and adventures, Paul was now employed by Dave Soleim, our long-time trusted friend. This was truly the hand of God, and even the Capstone Homes office was close to our house.

I had been an elementary school teacher in New Zealand for six years and thought I might work part-time as an instructional assistant until my credentials could be approved. This turned out to be easy, and I was employed at a local elementary school as a para-teacher for four hours a day.

Daniel was gone to a liberal arts college, and Sarah was going to Green River Community College to begin the first two years of her business degree. Jemima and Priscilla were enrolled in local schools. It was time for us to find a church that we could work in and enjoy.

We were looking for a church that felt like family, where we could grow spiritually and also serve using the gifts God had given us over the years.

No matter what church we have been to anywhere, we find that each one has its own culture and its own church politics. These issues can often be confused with Christianity. So many 'churched' people have been disillusioned about their faith because of rigid rules, hypocrisy, legalism, pastoral control, and church culture.

These issues have caused many people to toss out "the baby with the bathwater," and to have nothing more to do with God. Paul and I determined that we would develop our personal relationship with God and His Word, outside of dependency on organized religion.

Yes, churches are important for many reasons, including corporate worship, fellowship, support, and teaching about spiritual issues. However, anything learned must be applied personally before a person can grow spiritually and develop their relationship with God.

We knew that true faith was not about appearances or traditions—it was about living out the Word in our daily lives, walking with God in the quiet and the chaos alike.

We eventually found a church where we could not only worship freely but where we could serve and use our experience to support the pastor's work. I was a part-time paid counselor, as well as both Paul and I taking the evening services. It was a wonderful time there, for which we have so many amazing memories.

In 1992, we had lived in America for five years and were now able to apply to become American citizens. We could hardly wait to apply to the Immigration and Naturalization Service. Being an American had been a dream in our hearts since New Zealand, and now it was becoming a reality.

Everything about being a real American thrilled us. We wanted to be able to vote and understand the government. For years, we had been marveling at the words on coins— words like "Liberty" and "In God We Trust." The patriotism was amazing.

There was a feeling about America that we had never felt in New Zealand or Canada. Each Fourth of July filled us with awe, listening to the patriotic music and the renderings of the National Anthem, along with "Land That I Love" and "I'm Proud to Be an American."

We felt such a deep connection with the American dream—freedom, opportunity, and a nation built on values that resonated with our hearts. It was more than just a place to live—it felt like home.

The paperwork finally came in the mail. What a joy! There was information included that told us the application could take up to one year before the appointment to citizenship. Additional information was that we would need to take a test on both American history and American government.

A booklet was included for us to study, and we were also told that we would have to read and write a few sentences in English. Fortunately, this would not be a difficulty for us. A lot of time was spent looking up the Constitution and watching movies about American history and the Civil War.

Our excitement never waned at all. Paul and I quizzed each other on the history and government facts in the booklet, and I loved reading about the Statue of Liberty on Liberty Island in New York Harbor.

Every page we read made us more grateful. We weren't just gaining citizenship—we were gaining a deeper understanding of the country we had grown to love.

The year went by quickly, as we were always busy. We had a weekly home group meeting in our home. These meetings were wonderful. Everyone began to share and discuss the things that were on their heart. I provided snacks and coffee, etc., and relationships with the people who came were close.

One of the young men, Mike, who came, needed to use the bathroom during the evening. We always put Pete in his cage in the bath behind the shower curtain, so he wouldn't be a distraction. Apparently, while Mike was using the restroom, Pete heard him and chirped very loudly from behind the curtain, "Praise the Lord."

This definitely gave Mike a surprise, as he had no idea that Pete was behind the curtain!

That moment became a running joke in our home group. It reminded us all that praise could come in unexpected ways—and sometimes, through a tiny feathered messenger!

The all-important appointment time came in the mail for Paul and me to become American citizens. It was for October 1993. In the evenings, we brushed up on our test information and tested each other mercilessly. The night before our appointment, we looked out our best clothes for the occasion and made sure that our papers were ready.

This was going to be the fulfillment of a dream—a dream to become American!

We arrived at the United States Department of Justice in Seattle in plenty of time. Paul and I went through security and were shown into a waiting room. The atmosphere was tense, probably because of the anticipation of the occasion, and we were not the only ones there.

On this day, we were individually requested by authorities to go into a room. When they called my name, I was ready and had a wonderful peace. I felt the presence of the Lord with me.

I went into a room that was not much bigger than our living room at home. The entire back wall was a huge American flag, edged with gold. An officer showed me where to sit at a desk, and another armed officer stood at the back of the room. The door was closed for my appointment.

I was shown some paragraphs of writing and asked to read one of them. No additional conversation was permitted, and after reading, I was asked to write some sentences which the officer told me to write.

The next step was to stand and face the flag at the back of the room. The armed officer began asking me some of the test questions.

"Who said, 'Give me liberty or give me death'?"

"Patrick Henry," I replied.

The officer went on to ask me about the Boston Tea Party, branches of government, number of senators, and number of representatives. When the officer had finished asking me the test questions, she continued to ask me other questions, like "Would you be prepared to bear arms for the United States if necessary?"

After the questions were over, I was shown the Oath of Allegiance on a screen and asked to sign my agreement on some papers, by placing one hand on the Bible.

The whole time I was in that room, it felt very formal, official, and grand.

It was more than just a test—it was a sacred moment. I stood there with my heart full, realizing how far we had come. God had led us across oceans, through nations, and now, into the citizenship of the country we had prayed for.

Chapter 15.

American Citizens

The drive home was a time for reflection on the goodness of God. We would never have become Americans without our relationship with God and His provision of Scripture for us to believe in and act on. The Lord has never failed us.

It took eight years of trying, longing, hard work, and many adventures just to get to the point of living here as "Aliens" with green cards. Then, five more years passed before we could apply for citizenship, and one more year brought us to this special day—a total of fourteen years.

Reading and signing the Oath of Allegiance was a surreal experience. I felt better than royalty! Honestly, if I had been born in America, I would have missed out on this amazing, once-in-a-lifetime journey.

At the time of becoming an American citizen, I was still working part-time as an instructional assistant at an elementary school. The principal of the school, Mr. Fondren, was a military veteran. I told him the next day all about what Paul and I had just done—how we had finally become U.S. citizens.

To my surprise and joy, Mr. Fondren invited me to speak at the school's upcoming Veterans Day Assembly on November 10th. He asked if I could share my story with the students, teachers, and guests under the theme: "On Becoming a U.S. Citizen." I was thrilled, honored, and gladly agreed.

The assembly was held in the school gymnasium. It was such a special moment when Mr. Fondren invited our youngest daughter, Priscilla, to sing the National Anthem— "The Star-Spangled Banner"—right after the Pledge of Allegiance. She sang beautifully, and as I watched her, I couldn't help but remember the promise God gave me before she was born: that she would be "Lovely Songs." That promise was being fulfilled right before my eyes.

When it was my turn to speak, I shared how deeply I felt about America. I spoke about the sense of freedom, warmth, and acceptance I experienced here. I talked about something that happened just a few days earlier, while I was sitting in a doctor's waiting room.

There was only one other person there—an elderly man with one leg. He told me his leg had been blown off in Italy during World War II. As I looked at him, I saw someone who had suffered so much and paid a heavy price for the freedom

I now enjoy. I was moved to tears and said to him, "Thank you for all you've done and gone through. It's people like you who've made it possible for me to come to this land that I love."

The man broke down and cried. He told me that no one had ever said that to him before. Then he added, "If it was only for you, it was worth it to hear you say that."

His words touched me so deeply. I'll never forget that moment.

There were many veterans in the assembly that day. As I looked around the room, I felt overwhelmed with gratitude. I owe so much to them all—for their sacrifices, their courage, and their service.

Becoming a U.S. citizen was more than just paperwork or ceremony. It was a journey of faith, perseverance, and miracles. And on that day, sharing my story with others, I truly felt like I belonged—not just on paper, but in heart and spirit.

CHAPTER 16.

THE AMERICAN DREAM

Paul continued to work at Capstone Homes as a controller for many years. He was faithful, steady, and always gave his best. Meanwhile, I decided to further my education. I enrolled at Seattle Pacific University, studying at one of their satellite campuses to earn more credits toward an endorsement in Special Education.

Soon after, I began working as a teacher for grades seven, eight, and nine in a different school district. It was challenging at times, but incredibly rewarding. I loved working with the students and helping them discover their strengths, especially those who struggled in traditional classrooms. It felt like a calling, not just a job.

During this season, we built a home out in the country. It was peaceful, surrounded by nature, and full of the sounds of birds, wind in the trees, and—at our house—lots of barking. At one point, we had four dogs—two large and two small.

I've always had a deep love for Shepherds—both German and Dutch. There's just something noble and loyal about them. One of our dogs was a rescued Border Collie named Isaac. He had come from a heartbreaking background—he'd been starved and neglected, and it had left him with ongoing stomach problems. But Isaac was gentle, sweet, and blended beautifully with our little pack. He lived to be 13 years old. When he passed, we buried him under a grove of trees on our property, in a quiet spot where the sun shines through the branches. It felt like the right place.

But Isaac's passing affected our other dog, Max, in a way we hadn't expected. Max was a German Shepherd–Doberman mix—strong, intelligent, and protective. But after Isaac was gone, Max sat by his grave all day. He refused to eat, and we could see the sadness in his eyes. It broke our hearts.

Our vet tried everything—different treatments, medications, and advice—but nothing worked. Finally, he suggested that we get another dog, something to distract Max and maybe help him heal.

I told Paul that I really wanted a Dutch Shepherd. I loved their strength, their guarding instincts, and especially their beautiful brindle-colored coats. So, we reached out to a breeder. But the breeder wasn't encouraging. He told us that Dutch Shepherds were best suited for police work or search and rescue missions. They were intense and high-energy—not ideal as house pets.

We weren't sure what to do, so we decided to pray. I asked the Lord for wisdom and guidance. I asked Him to provide the right dog—if there was one out there that was just meant for us. I told God I still hoped for a Dutch Shepherd, but only if it was safe and truly "pet quality."

A few days later, I called the breeder again. He was kind but firm. He said, "A German Shepherd is like a butter knife. A Dutch Shepherd is a steak knife." He warned us again—don't get one unless it's specifically bred for home life.

At that point, I started to lose hope. So I turned to rescue organizations and started applying for German Shepherds instead. But oddly enough, every single application fell through. Either the timing didn't work, or the rescue organizations didn't approve of our property because the front fence was too low.

I started to wonder—was God closing every door on purpose?

So I asked Paul to pray with me again, specifically for a "pet quality" Dutch Shepherd. I believed that if God wanted us to have one, He could find the right match.

After that prayer, I went on the PetFinder website and typed in "Dutch Shepherd." Right away, a picture popped up on my phone—a gorgeous brindle-colored Dutch Shepherd, brown and gold, with bright eyes and a noble face. My heart leapt. What a beauty!

I thought the dog was in Arizona because of the blurred initials on the picture. I quickly called the number listed and spoke to a kind woman named Kim. She told me the dog wasn't in Arizona—it was in Arkansas! Kim ran a rescue ranch and said she never flew dogs to Seattle, especially if it meant changing planes.

But something about our conversation felt different— like it was meant to be. Kim told me that this dog had been found abandoned, along with two Pit Bulls, on a deserted property that had once been a drug house. The place had been left to rot, and the dogs had been surviving on their own.

Apparently, the owner of the dogs had been taken to prison, and the animals were left unattended for quite some time. A woman walking her own dogs happened to pass by the abandoned property. She noticed the dogs and reported the situation to the police. Thankfully, the authorities responded. All three dogs—two Pit Bulls and the Dutch

Shepherd—were taken to the hospital for care and rehabilitation, and when they were healthy enough, they were transferred to various rescue organizations.

The Dutch Shepherd ended up at Kim's rescue ranch. She was the one who had advertised the dog for adoption.

Shortly after arriving, the town's Search and Rescue officer came to evaluate the Dutch Shepherd to see if she might qualify for work. These dogs are often used in highly trained rescue missions, and the officer wanted to see if she had potential.

But the poor dog had recently given birth to puppies and was still recovering, both physically and emotionally. She failed all the tests. After that, the officer decided he didn't want her. She didn't fit the criteria for working dogs.

That's when Kim and I really connected. She asked me, "Why do you want a Dutch Shepherd?"

I told her the story of Isaac—how we had rescued him, how he had passed, and how Max was grieving deeply. I explained how we had prayed specifically for a Dutch Shepherd—not just any dog, but one that would fit our family and help Max heal. I poured out my heart.

Kim listened quietly and then said, "You must be a Christian."

I smiled and said, "Yes, we are."

She went on to tell me that she was also a Christian. Every two weeks, she met with a group of other Christian dog lovers from different churches. Together, they would pray for the dogs on her no-kill ranch, asking God to place each one in the perfect home.

Then she said something that touched me deeply: "Why don't you send me pictures of your property, and when we meet next with the group, we'll pray and consider if it's possible to get this dog to you."

I was overwhelmed—in the best way. The Lord really does have amazing ways of answering prayer and giving favor.

A little while later, Kim called me back with wonderful news. She said the prayer group had met, and after seeing the photos and hearing the story, every single person agreed that this dog would be going to a home where she would live in splendor. They believed she was meant to be with us.

Even though Kim had noticed our fence was low, she said, "This dog doesn't like to jump. She's gentle. Definitely pet quality."

The group that had prayed over the dog included the local head of the Humane Society. He generously offered to provide the travel crate for the journey.

Another member was the wife of a doctor who worked at the Joplin Hospital. She volunteered to drive the dog five hours to the Dallas-Fort Worth Airport and personally ensure she made it onto the flight to Seattle. After dropping her off, she was even willing to drive the five hours back home that same night.

Others in the group helped in different ways. Kim took the dog to the vet to get all her health checks and paperwork in order for the trip. Everyone played a part.

Of course, we reimbursed them for their time and costs—but the love, effort, and kindness they showed us will always be priceless. Kim and I have remained friends ever since.

When our new dog arrived, we named her Joy—because she came into our lives as a gift from God, replacing the sorrow we felt after losing Isaac.

We've now had Joy for eight wonderful years. She's every bit a guard dog—alert, smart, and protective—but she's also sweet and calm. She has never once jumped the fence. In fact, she's so cautious that when it's time to get in the car, we actually have to lift her back legs into the hatchback. There's nothing wrong with her—she just believes she can't jump. And honestly, we don't mind. That's just Joy.

She's truly *pet quality*—and a living, furry reminder of God's ability to answer even the most specific prayers. God loves faith. And He loves when we believe He can do the impossible.

During my teaching career, I also wrote a curriculum for a passion-based writing course called "Man's Best Friend." It was all about dogs, and students were always excited to sign up. That class was a hit every year—it connected students' love for animals with creativity and learning. I loved teaching it.

Eventually, I had the opportunity to teach American History, and I enjoyed every single minute of it. I poured my heart into that class, not just teaching facts, but helping my students understand the privilege of being American—and the deep responsibility that comes with that privilege.

CHAPTER 17.

THE MIRACLE OF THE KEYS----
ADVENTURES IN AMERICA

At some point in America, I knew we would run into a timeshare salesperson. We met several over time and narrowly escaped by choosing to vacation with a travel trailer. Paul could haul the trailer with his truck, and we were able to park it at the front of our property.

The benefit of the trailer idea was that we could bring the dogs with us and not have to put them into boarding kennels. It made every trip feel more personal and homely.

Besides, I loved the dollhouse feeling I had when I set up the inside of the trailer after arriving at our campground. I appreciated how easy it was to stock up the fridge in the trailer when it was on our property.

To be ready for the upcoming camping weekend, I went to Costco to get supplies. My cart was full of frozen food, and I was in a hurry to put my purchases in the car.

For the first time ever, I couldn't find my keys. My key ring was a heavy one because it had the house keys, the car keys, and the post office key all on the ring. My handbag was fairly soft, and I couldn't feel the key ring.

Of course, I went through every pocket and zip compartment, but the keys were not there. I looked under the car and wondered if my keys had fallen down one of those wide drains.

I would have noticed if I had somehow dropped them, because I always put the keys into my bag after locking the car.

I began to panic because I had left my cell phone in the car console, and I needed to get the frozen food home. I sat on the ground outside my car to go through my handbag again. Tears were beginning to fill my eyes.

It's funny how even the smallest things can feel overwhelming when you're in a rush. But in moments like this, faith becomes real and powerful.

This is what is wonderful about knowing the Lord, and having the understanding that He is a very present help in time of trouble. I prayed and asked the Lord to please help me find my keys.

While I was still praying, a voice said to me, "You seem upset, dear."

I replied that I was, and that I couldn't find my keys. I looked up briefly to see who had spoken, and I saw a woman in a purple dress.

I continued to look around under the car when the woman said, "Look again in your handbag."

By now, I had looked so many times in my bag, and besides, there was nothing left in it. However, I did as the lady said and looked again in my empty handbag.

There were my keys—in a heavy lump at the bottom of my bag. I knew this was something supernatural.

I looked up to thank the woman, but she was totally gone.

Not just out of sight—completely vanished. I stood there stunned, heart racing, holding my keys, because now they were a miracle.

I gathered up my bag contents from the ground and I knew, without a doubt, that the woman must have been an angel.

This particular weekend felt special because of the keys incident. We decided to go to a campground in Washington, which had a very modern clubhouse.

The dogs loved coming with us and meeting other dogs at the campground.

Every Saturday, the clubhouse would put on breakfast for the campers for just five dollars. It was a great time to meet other people and share ideas.

There was a sense of community that made everything feel warmer and more inviting.

On this occasion, we were parked beside another couple with their camper. Jill and Ben had been camping a week before we arrived beside them. It was good to get to know them.

When Saturday came, we decided to go to the clubhouse for breakfast and invited our new neighbors to come with us.

Jill and Ben had a dog and cat with them, and we all left our animals inside our trailers and walked together to the clubhouse.

The kitchen at the clubhouse was set with long tables to accommodate several people. Paul and I sat opposite Jill and Ben. There were a few other people at the same table.

After we had eaten our breakfast, Jill said to those around us, "Has anyone got a story to share?"

I piped up, "Yes, I do."

"Okay then, let's hear it," Ben said.

I proceeded to tell the people at the table about my keys—which had gone missing just a couple of days before.

Jill sat silent for a few seconds, just staring at me. Then she said, "You're not going to believe this, but when we left our camper to walk with you to breakfast, we locked our key inside the camper. Each of us thought the other had the key. Neither of us had a spare."

She paused. "Since God helped you to find your keys, would you pray for us—that God will help us find ours?"

We said we would love to.

A man sitting further down the table had been listening to this. He spoke up and said, "I'm a Catholic, but I'd like to join you and pray with you."

Paul told him, "The more, the better."

There was something beautiful about strangers uniting in faith. In that moment, we weren't different denominations—we were just people asking God for help.

The five of us left the clubhouse and walked to our neighbors' camper. We stood outside, and Paul prayed aloud.

Jill and Ben were concerned about their animals inside, who were anxiously looking out the window.

Paul went to get a tool and began fiddling with it in the keyhole of their door.

Meanwhile, the Catholic man had gone to the back of the camper for a few minutes. He returned holding a small black box in his hand.

"Look what I found under the bumper," he said.

It was a magnetic lock box.

Jill and Ben looked at the man in shock. Ben opened the box—and inside was a key that fit the camper door perfectly.

It was like time stopped for a second. None of us could believe it.

Jill burst into tears and said she had never had an answer to prayer like that before.

Ben added that they had bought the camper used about two years earlier—and had no idea there was a lock box on it.

We all stood around talking about what had happened. It was beyond wonderful.

Later that afternoon, Jill and Ben went into town and came back with a small gift: a lock box for Paul and me.

That little gesture said everything. Gratitude. Faith. Friendship.

We had many wonderful trips in our trailer.

There is something amazing about being happy together.

It is a peace that money cannot buy.

Camping wasn't just about the places we visited—it was about the people, the quiet moments, the sense of contentment that came with living simply.

Having a personal relationship with the Lord—and maintaining it through prayer, worship, and reading God's Word—is what provides this peace within us.

During this time, our family continued to worship at the church where I was working as a part-time counselor.

Our family had grown, and each one was making their own way in life.

Sarah earned a degree in Business Administration. She was working as a Court Clerk and Real Estate investor.

Daniel was enjoying being a software architect, focused on cloud and AI technologies. He has been granted thirty patents and has twenty more pending.

Jemima was living a very busy life as a successful attorney.

Priscilla earned her Bachelor of Nursing Science, and continues loving being a nurse.

All four of our children have successful families and love being American citizens.

It fills our hearts with gratitude to see them thriving, rooted in faith and values.

Growing our relationship with the Lord personally—and with His Word—is key to the way God has blessed us.

We are not New Zealand Americans, neither are we Canadian Americans.

We are just American in heart and spirit, loving what this country stands for:

One Nation under God, indivisible, with liberty and justice for all.

EPILOGUE

If you've made it this far, thank you for walking this road with us.

We didn't set out to write a perfect story—just a *real* one. A story of a family who dared to believe that God still speaks, still leads, and still answers prayer. Through every twist, every delay, every unexpected blessing—we've come to see something clearly:

God is always faithful.

We've learned that faith doesn't mean everything will be easy. It means trusting when things *don't* make sense, when doors close, and when the wait feels long. It means holding on when all you have is a promise from the Word, and the knowledge that nothing is impossible with God. And it means staying thankful, even when the road gets bumpy.

But oh, what a journey it's been.

From New Zealand to Canada, from Canada to America—from visas to valleys, from homes to heartaches, and from dreams to divine appointments—we've been carried by grace every step of the way. And we believe the same can be true for you.

Maybe you're waiting for your own door to open. Maybe you're facing your own flood or hoping for your own "Joy." Whatever season you're in, just remember:

God loves you.

He hasn't forgotten you, and He's not finished writing your story. So keep believing what Romans 8 v 37 says, 'In all these things, we are more than conquerors through Him who loves us". Keep praying. Keep praising—even when the cage topples over.

And when you least expect it, don't be surprised if something—or *Someone*—shows up in your passenger seat, reminding you that you're never alone.

Thank you for being a part of our journey.

With all our hearts,

We pray your journey is full of purpose, peace, and the beautiful relationship only God can give.

ABOUT THE AUTHOR

Delwyn Beveridge loves sharing with groups the many adventures she and her husband, Paul, have experienced on their journey from New Zealand to the United States. Often asked questions like, "Why did you leave New Zealand?" or "What brought you here?" Delwyn enjoys recounting the heartfelt stories behind their move. A passionate dog lover with a background in teaching and ministry, Delwyn weaves her family's journey into compelling narratives that are sure to touch your heart.

www.ingramcontent.com/pod-product-compliance
Lightning Source LLC
Chambersburg PA
CBHW051316120626
46547CB00015B/2256